TEN DER NESS

"*Tenderness* is a thoroughly encouraging reminder that the lives of traditionalist gay Christians, though sometimes marked by pain and rejection, often serve as stark examples of the beauty and dignity of redemption. With her characteristic wit and earthy humor, Eve Tushnet sheds light on obstacles that many non-straight Christians face in their lives while highlighting both the beauty and significance of faithful obedience to the Word of God. Although directed to traditionalist gay Christians themselves, anybody who wants to follow in the footsteps of Jesus will be encouraged by the testimony of our Father's tender faithfulness that inspires this book."

Nate Collins
Author of *All But Invisible*

"With grace, hope, and the conversational style of grabbing coffee with an old friend, Eve Tushnet has built upon her work in *Gay and Catholic* in a timely and desperately needed manner. She offers an abundant vision of the tender love of Jesus and the expansive ways in which we can receive that love."

Bekah Mason
Executive director of Revoice

"*Tenderness* is a book so open, insightful, wry, and generous that I devoured it in one sitting and wished it was longer. By turns hilarious, frank, heartbreaking, and ultimately hopeful, it is an inspired, irresistible read that manages to instruct without injuring and makes us long to bring about the world Eve Tushnet can see so clearly."

Elizabeth Scalia
Editor at-large at Word on Fire Catholic Ministries
and author of *Strange Gods*

"There is no one who writes about the particular gifts and challenges of being gay and Christian with more prophetic insight, godly wisdom, humane sensitivity, and sheer good humor than Eve Tushnet. This book will be a candle in the dark for many gay believers who wonder whether the promises of the Gospel really are for them, and it will help others in the Church see the beauty of God's image in the faces of his beloved gay children. This is now the best guide in print for those of us who know ourselves to be gay and want to live a life of faith and hope in the love of God in Christ."

Wesley Hill
Author of *Spiritual Friendship: Finding Love in the Church as a Celibate Gay Christian*

"If 'the truth will set you free,' why do many gay people find Christian life anxious and burdensome? If churches are communities of mercy, why do they often strike outsiders as judgmental? To anyone interested in these questions, *Tenderness* is essential reading. It's also a brilliant piece of writing about the ups and downs of the spiritual life—brutally honest, painfully funny, and suffused with hope."

Dan Hitchens
Reporter at the *Catholic Herald*

"For decades, so many of our gay sisters and brothers have been hurt by words of disappointment and even disgust coming from the very Church they love. They have been told that the welcoming embrace of Christ and tender love of God the Father was not theirs to fall into. This reality should break our hearts and inspire us to work to become a Church that revives our gay sister's and brother's trust in God. Eve Tushnet's *Tenderness* is the honest, fearless, transformative roadmap to help us achieve that goal. It's a hope-filled message that has the potential to save lives and lead souls to Christ."

Tommy Tighe
Author of *St. Dymphna's Playbook*

TEN DER NESS

A Gay Christian's Guide to Unlearning Rejection
and Experiencing God's Extravagant Love

Eve Tushnet

AVE MARIA PRESS AVE Notre Dame, Indiana

Founded in 1865, Ave Maria Press is a ministry of the United States Province of Holy Cross.

www.avemariapress.com

Paperback: ISBN-13 978-1-64680-074-2

E-book: ISBN-13 978-1-64680-075-9

Cover image © Ekely / Getty Images.

Cover and text design by Brianna Dombo.

Printed and bound in the United States of America.

Library of Congress Cataloging-in-Publication Data
Names: Tushnet, Eve, author.
Title: Tenderness : a gay Christian's guide to unlearning rejection and experiencing God's extravagant love / Eve Tushnet.
Description: Notre Dame, Indiana : Ave Maria Press, [2021] | Includes bibliographical references. | Summary: "In Tenderness, Eve Tushnet offers hope and companionship for gay Christians who have been hurt by their churches and feel cut off from God. Tushnet shares the tools that helped her find a place in Catholicism as a celibate lesbian, and offers practical guidance from her own journey of learning to trust God's love"-- Provided by publisher.
Identifiers: LCCN 2021032644 (print) | LCCN 2021032645 (ebook) | ISBN 9781646800742 (paperback) | ISBN 9781646800759 (ebook)
Subjects: LCSH: Christian gays--Religious life. | God (Christianity)--Love. | Catholic Church--Doctrines. | BISAC: RELIGION / Christianity / General | RELIGION / Christian Living / Social Issues
Classification: LCC BV4596.G38 T87 2021 (print) | LCC BV4596.G38 (ebook) | DDC 261.8/35766--dc23
LC record available at https://lccn.loc.gov/2021032644
LC ebook record available at https://lccn.loc.gov/2021032645

For eternal blessedness consists of this:
knowing God as He really is.
–Sigrid Undset, *Catherine of Siena*

I did not love you as a joke.
–the words of Jesus to
Bl. Angela of Foligno in a vision

CONTENTS

Introduction

HER MISTRESS'S HAND

"Oh, I wasn't raised Catholic, so I don't have all that baggage."[1]

I used to say that a lot. I converted in 1998, at age nineteen, having come out as a lesbian when I was about thirteen. My parents and most of the people in my world were secular progressives. Even the people who brought me into the Church, who first taught me who Jesus is and what the love of God is like, didn't make a big deal out of my sexual orientation. Maybe to some of them it made me a little bit exotic; maybe to some of them it made me a little bit of a mess. (I was *a lot* of a mess . . . though not because I was gay.) But all of them treated me like any other person they knew. They talked to me about the Incarnation and the Crucifixion, instead of thinking they needed to start off by making sure I knew what Jesus thought of my sex life.

The Catholic sexual ethic, in which (among other things) sex is restricted to marriage between a man and a woman, was probably the biggest obstacle for me when I was trying to figure out if I really needed to knuckle under and become Catholic. I sought various explanations of this teaching from friends—and from a well-meaning, unhelpful priest—but none of the explanations I received then persuaded me. They still don't. I have a better sense now of how Catholic teaching fits into the patterns of scripture, which you'll see a bit of in this book, but in reality the Church's sexual ethic is still something I take on trust rather than because I've been convinced by some argument about it.

Still, I longed for the Eucharist, and I knew that if I was confirmed in the Church, I'd be asked to affirm that I believed all that the Catholic Church teaches to be true. My friends had presented the Church to me as beauty and rescue, not a bunch of rules for good behavior. But I accepted the Church's own account of herself, in which the morality was not separable from the beauty and the rescue. I was being asked to trust the Catholic Church as both mother and teacher: a mother who would nourish me with Jesus' Body and Blood, and a teacher who would show me Jesus the Way—a way of life, which I was to follow even when I didn't understand.

Much to my surprise and dismay, I found that I *did* have that trust.[2]

This is an admittedly oversimplified account, but it should make clear how different my experience was from that of most gay people in our churches. I met gay people first as my parents' friends, then as my own community. They were never threats or even strangers. I didn't have to worry that the people who had taught me to know Jesus would reject me if I came out to them, because I was out already. I didn't have to suspect that Christian sexual morality was just an excuse for straight people to reject us and indulge their bigotry, because most of the straight Christians I knew were genuinely interested in listening to me and willing to correct any misunderstandings they had about gay people and communities.

I was still damaged by the silence and homophobia within our churches. When I became Catholic, I didn't know *of* anyone—let alone know someone personally—who was openly gay and accepted the Church's sexual ethic. I made a lot of mistakes, often sinful mistakes, due not only to my own weaknesses but to the bad guidance I received, as well as to my refusal to hear the witness of other gay people. Don't worry—I'll talk about all that stuff later in this book.

But I was able to escape a lot of the shame and fear that gay people who grew up Christian often experience. I never—seriously, not once—believed that God loved me less or cherished me less because I'm gay. I'm not sure I've ever met a cradle Catholic who can say that.

One day I overheard myself saying that cute line about how little baggage I have as a convert. For the first time I realized what I was really saying, and it shocked me. I was saying that it's typically easier for a gay person who grows up outside the Church to know God's love than for a gay person who had a Catholic upbringing. The children of the Church, who should be the *most* confident in God's love, the ones who know best what God is like, are instead the ones who grow up uncertain of God's love and afraid that there's no place for them in the Church.

Gay people who seek to submit our lives to God's guidance through the Church are like the maidservant in Psalm 123:

> Like the eyes of a maid
>   on the hand of her mistress,
> So our eyes are on the LORD our God,
>   till we are shown favor. (Ps 123:2)[3]

We look to the hand of our mistress, the Bride of Christ—the Church—to know what we are to do and where we are to go. We long to go where she points us. But what is the character of this mistress? What is our Mother and Teacher *like*?

Even (especially?) gay people who have always tried to do right and be good Christian kids often wake up one day in their twenties or thirties and realize that they have never really believed that God cherished them. They have always felt, on some level, that God was disgusted by them and did not delight in them the way he delighted in people with more conventional desires. They knew intellectually—they accepted, as a dogma of their faith—that God loved them; but they pictured it as a dutiful love, colored by that familiar parental admixture of expectations and disappointment.

Gay people who grow up Christian so often learn the following lessons:

- their sexuality separates them from God;
- obedience is impossible for them unless they become straight;
- not solely their sexual desires but their longings for love and intimacy are fundamentally broken, intrinsically disordered;
- there is no history of gay followers of Jesus and therefore no guidance for their futures;
- gay communities must be avoided as petri dishes of sexual sin;
- gay people are uniquely difficult to love and even accepting us is a real struggle.

And this teaches gay Christians that God is not on our side. This teaches us that the Church is a mother who rejects us and abandons us when we need her most. We find ourselves obedient to a mistress who holds us in contempt and punishes us mercilessly, arbitrarily, and forbids us even to speak about what we've experienced at her hands.

So many of us have been taught a model of obedience that is really a form of self-harm.

This is not God, and this is not God's Church.

In this book I will explore gay Christians' need for the tenderness of God. I'll look at the many ways our churches have given us false images of God and the damage this has done to our faith. Because we are made in the image of God, a false image of God necessarily becomes a false image of oneself. A cruel God produces a degraded creature defined by its sins. Because God is Love, a false image of God necessarily becomes a false idea of love. The lines between love and harm, humility and self-hatred, become blurred and can even vanish.

But there is good news. By examining scripture, Christian history, and the everyday lives of gay people in the churches, we can discover the true nature of the God who is Love. We can learn to see our neighbor and ourselves with his tender gaze. I will explore the ways God shows his tenderness to us, even when we least expect it: in our longings for same-sex intimacy and love, in our times of doubt or anger, even in our experiences of sin and shame. And I will suggest a few—only a few, since a comprehensive list would be impossible—practical ways by which individual gay believers have deepened our intimacy with Christ and experienced more fully his ardent love.

What if gay people were *safer* in our churches than in the secular world? What if we could find *more* ways to give and receive love within the Church than we do outside it? If this seems impossible, it only shows how far we have strayed from the path the Lord has called us to walk.

My hope is that this book will contribute to an ongoing transformation in gay Christians' lives and in our churches—a transformation in which we begin to see the mistakes we've made in the past, with which almost all of us have been in some way complicit, and rediscover the sweetness of God's love for his gay children. This transformation will mostly start with gay and same-sex attracted people ourselves and those who have sought to stand alongside us, but it will ripple out through the Body of Christ and renew our understandings of kinship, friendship, celibacy and unmarried life, ordered love, personal integrity, solidarity with the marginalized, obedience, surrender, sanctification, and hope. This transformation has already begun; I'm just trying to make it go faster. Already gay Christians, in our nascent communities, are working to revive gay people's trust in God—a trust our shepherds have too often damaged or even killed, but which our tender and good Shepherd can restore to life.

We can come to know Jesus as our greatest Lover and most intimate Friend, who will never leave our side or turn against us, no matter how far we try to go from him. We can come to know God the Father as one who loves us in a way even the best earthly parents can't, whose love for us flows from delight and not from duty—a Father who cherishes us most lovingly when our paths to holiness startle, confuse, and disappoint our own parents. And we can come to know the Church as a sweet mistress whose hand always points the way to greater love. We will still, always, be called to sacrifice: to lay down our lives, to give everything and hold back nothing for ourselves. But our sacrifices can be both fruit and seedbed of trusting love, not self-loathing shame.

The thesis of this book, which guides its structure, is that God offers himself and his ardent love to his gay children, and he offers us as gifts to our churches and loved ones—but Christians have made it unnecessarily hard for gay people to trust in God's tenderness. Thus even—especially—gay people who grew up loving God often need to rediscover him, uncovering his hidden, tender face.

I begin by looking at the experiences that have hidden God's sweetness from his gay children. This is a difficult topic to read about. I'm starting with it because this is where most actual gay Christians start out: in the gap between "God is Love" and "For the sake of the children, we're going to have to ask you to leave." Some people hear harsh words from the pulpit (in the school hallways, on the street, at the church coffee hour, in therapy, in a meeting with your supervisor or your pastor; at home). Others hear only a blank and deadly silence. Insults, well-intentioned falsehoods, and echoing absences all teach people what it is to be gay in the churches.

If you've experienced any of these harms, I hope this first chapter will make clear that you aren't alone. You weren't harmed in

Christian communities because you're unusually lacking in faith—
or even just unusually unlucky. Your painful experiences are part of
a shockingly common pattern. You don't have to wallow in them,
but being able to see the pattern may relieve any self-blame you
feel and help you articulate which aspects of your relationship with
God need healing.

If your experience has been much gentler, you aren't alone
either. My own experience in the Catholic Church has been *very*
gentle. That gives me a lot of hope that none of these harms are
necessary! But this first chapter is also for people like me, who have
been spared many of these harms. I hope to give people a better
sense of what others have been through, so that they can avoid
some of the mistakes I made out of naivete. And it's possible that
you will find, as I did, that you didn't escape quite as unscathed as
you thought.

The rest of the book will offer an alternative curriculum—a way
of unlearning all these hard, familiar lessons.

In the second section, I look at two experiences many of us
were taught to view as isolating, loveless, or even sinful: same-sex
love and celibacy. If you are afraid that your same-sex longings can
only be loathed and fled, in the second chapter you may discover
the ways in which God can use these longings to illuminate your
path. If you are afraid that the only words scripture has to say about
your longings are "abomination" and "against nature," I hope I can
suggest that same-sex love is woven into the history of our salvation. If you have ever prayed to become straight because it seemed
like that was the only way you could be pleasing to God, this second
chapter will suggest ways of bringing order to your desires while
still remaining, you know, extra gay.

Most gay people who seek to follow the Catholic sexual ethic
will live celibately. If you have considered a life without sexual relationships but feel despair when you think about a future of empty
evenings, microwaveable meals-for-one, and Netflix alone, the third
chapter will look at the vision and promise of Christian celibacy.

In the New Testament, celibacy is a way of life that offers unique freedom to love and unique forms of witness to God's faithfulness. This chapter will look at what it means to live a celibate life of beauty and self-giving love, even—especially!—when you didn't choose it and didn't feel "called" to it.

Same-sex love and celibacy are both so much better than you've probably been taught. But other experiences are about as bad as you think they are, maybe even worse, and the third section explores these genuinely awful experiences: spiritual abuse, familial abandonment, rage at the harm that Christian homophobia has done to you, sexual shame, ambivalence about your faith, and other forms of suffering. I hope these chapters will offer hope, grounded in scripture, Christian history, and experience. God is with you in these times, too, and still offers you shelter and support.

If you have experienced abandonment or abuse within Christian churches or Christian homes, chapter 4 will seek to walk with you as you examine the injustices you endured. Scripture reveals, again and again, that God is on your side. If you're afraid of the anger that wells up inside you when you start confronting what others have done to you, or if you're eaten up by guilt when you think about the rotten things you did in response to fear and shame, chapter 5 will show you how other gay Christians have felt the same things—and through them arrived at a deeper confidence in God's just and gentle love.

If you've felt intense shame over your sexuality, or over your sexual sins, the sixth chapter will shine the light of God's mercy in those places. This chapter will offer everything from ancient Christian theology to practical advice on habit formation. The intimacy you offer God during times of shame and sin is an especially profound intimacy, reflecting an especially deep trust. He will not reject it.

And if you've felt doubt and ambivalence about Christianity or the Christian sexual ethic, the seventh chapter will explore this extremely normal part of the life of faith. Ambivalence is part of almost every story of change; you are very likely to encounter it as you grow and mature in your faith.

And in the last chapter of this section, I'll look briefly at suffering. (Woo-hoo!) Most of this book focuses on alleviating the suffering caused by injustice or silence and showing you the beauty of the life Christ offers you. Even this eighth chapter is mostly about the ways Christians misinterpret gay people's suffering. But it's also necessary to say a few words about the cross of each believer—and the forms of suffering that are more common for gay Christians, not all of which are solely the result of individual or structural sin.

Each of these chapters will offer multiple ways of understanding your hard experiences. But I am not trying to exhaust all the possibilities! There are as many ways to come to know God's tenderness as there are people he created. Within the Catholic Church alone, there are more spiritual paths to God than I can count: Some people live a more Carmelite spirituality, while others love the Franciscan or the Jesuit or the Dominican way. Some will look to the traditions of the Eastern Christian churches, or the Catholic churches rooted in black American experience. My own spirituality is pretty much, "What if you love the 12 Steps, but refuse to go to meetings?" Whether your spirituality is more Gregorian chant or "Ride On, King Jesus" or Johnny Cash growling "Hurt," there is a way for you to come to Christ's embrace. I explore some of them here, on the theory that this will help you with your own exploration.

The final section of the book provides specific practices or ways of thinking that you can adopt in order to know God's tenderness for you as a gay believer. It's a little of everything, based on what my friends and I have found helpful. Nobody needs to do all of them, but most of us could probably stand to do some of them. Some of these practices will make you more obviously gay. Some of them will make you more flamboyantly Christian. All of them are intended to help you know God as he truly is and to rejoice that he knows you as you truly are.

You may notice that some of these chapters are super long ("Order in Same-Sex Love" could've been twice the length, I have *so much* to say about this!) and others quite short ("Ambivalence"). I've tried not to waste your time: I say what I think needs to be said, especially the things I haven't seen in books before, and then I stop talking. Bear with me through the inevitable structural inelegance.

A few notes about terminology. I mostly say *gay* here to describe myself and the people for whom this book is especially intended. I'll also say *lesbian* for the ladies. There are issues specific to bisexual Christians' experiences which I don't address, but I think much of what *is* here will be relevant to bi readers. Some of you all may prefer the term *same-sex attracted*; I think you'll find this book relevant to your experience as well. I'll sometimes say "gay or same-sex attracted," just to remind us that we're all in this together, but the places where I use that term aren't the only places where our needs and experiences are shared. And although I don't use it much because this book doesn't attempt to address questions specific to gender identity, I use *LGBT* here and there, when talking about communities where many members would use that term.

I definitely mess around with the word *celibacy*. Often, especially in Catholic circles, this word implies that someone has taken a vow renouncing marriage, consecrating themselves to God in the unmarried state. I'm using it more loosely, for people who are unmarried *and intending to remain unmarried*, whether or not they've made any vow. This isn't *singleness*. Nobody is single (God is our Lover! Sorry, I know this is a hobbyhorse of mine). Plenty of unmarried people want to marry and are either pursuing marriage or eager to accept a spouse if one appears; these people aren't "celibate" in the sense I'm using the word here. I'm also not using "celibacy" to mean *chastity*, which is simply the integrity—the harmony between flesh and spirit—we receive when, by God's grace, we obey Christian sexual discipline. You can be married and chaste, and you can be celibate and unchaste (ask me how I know . . .). Chapter 3 looks at celibacy, while chapter 6 looks at chastity.

I am still seeking an elegant phrase for "the Christian teaching that sex is restricted to marriage between a man and a woman." In this book I've used a lot of not-quite-right phrases to approximate this long, clunky phrase: "the Christian sexual ethic" or "the Catholic sexual ethic" or "Christian sexual discipline" (even though all of those phrases encompass *a lot* more than just restricting sex to opposite-sex marriage!). I don't mean to imply that all Christian churches, or all individual believers, accept this sexual ethic; I know many sincere followers of Jesus have rejected it. I've sometimes resorted to "traditional," even though the important thing about this belief is not that it's old but that it's a part of our faith, given to us not by our ancestors but by God.

And finally, I say *the Church* when I mean the Catholic Church—and especially her mystical aspect, the Church as the Bride of Christ and our Mother and Teacher. When I mean the often unmystical, all-too-often un-Christlike experiences Christians in every church inflict on one another, I'll say "the churches."

My hope is that twenty or thirty years down the line, I will be listening to some young whippersnapper who will say, with no idea that she's saying anything unusual, "Oh, I was raised Christian—so of course I've never doubted that God loved gay people."

Of course. Why should it ever have been different?

Now let's begin the long journey from this hard present to that future. Come and see how the Lord delights in his gay children.

Part I

HARD TIMES

one

THE GAY CHRISTIAN DRINKING GAME

Look, I could tell you a bunch of sad stories to convince you that the treatment gay people have received in our churches has warped our view of God and of ourselves as creatures made in God's image. But that kind of chapter would risk descending into misery porn, or lugubrious self-pity, and anyway it sounds like no fun, just more slogging for people who really need relief.

So let me instead offer an exercise in gallows humor. I am a recovering alcoholic; by God's unexpected mercy I've been freed from the destructive habits that go along with alcoholism, but I have not been freed from the fun habits, like thinking of everything in terms of a drinking game. So that's what I did here. I hope that things that are funny to me will also be funny to more well-adjusted people.

The following game is composed entirely of true stories: things that really happened to gay Christians I know, people who accepted their church's sexual ethic and sought to be obedient to it. Almost all of them happened to several people. Some of them happened to a majority of us.

Obviously, don't actually, you know, play this as a drinking game. Even at the height (or sticky depth) of my tolerance for booze, this game would've sent me to the hospital.[1] But as you knock back your shots of grape juice, or whatever, you may still find your vision blurring as a distorted and monstrous figure slowly appears, flickering on the edges of sight: the hallucinated version of

God, which is one symptom of long-term addiction to American Christianity.

The good news is, that god isn't real.

The bad news is, I bet a lot of you still see him when you close your eyes.

Take a drink if . . .

- the only time you ever heard the word "gay" from the pulpit, growing up, it was about how the gays are destroying America. If you want to get wrecked before the game really even gets going, do a shot for every single sermon you heard that set up gay people as enemies of the faith.
- as far as you knew you were the only person in history to be Christian and gay.
- the only advice you got about your future as a gay person in the Church was, "Don't worry, it's probably just a phase."[2]
- you've made homophobic jokes, or laughed at other people's, so that nobody would guess.
- you've developed a mysterious physical ailment, a fun stress-re-lated thing like eczema or ulcers, maybe something especially embarrassing like paruresis, maybe insomnia or panic attacks, which mysteriously started to get better when you finally gave up and came out.[3] (If you're still struggling with this ailment or its aftereffects, feel free to *drain your drink*. You've earned it.)
- some of the people you care about most stopped speaking to you when they found out you were gay,
- and your mother cried.
- you've desperately prayed to become straight, night after night, often in tears—with novenas, prayers to Our Lady Undoer of Knots, or whatever Protestants do when they *really, really need help*—and then after years of this, when you finally come out, straight Christians tell you that God will heal you if you just trust him.

- you've tried reparative therapy, healing prayer, reconciling with your father, punching a pillow, growing your hair long (for the ladies) or learning to throw a football (for the dudes), spending a weekend in the woods with other hot, young, confused, same-sex attracted guys (boy, *that* didn't go the way you intended), getting in touch with your feelings, learning to ignore your feelings, telling your most shameful personal secrets to an auditorium full of people,[4] going on dates with the opposite sex and frankly leading them on in ways you're now ashamed of; you've tried 12-step recovery from homosexuality, exorcism (twice), and a forty-day juice fast; and when you tell your straight[5] Christian friend that you're still super gay, she says, "Have you read Leanne Payne?[6] I think her approach could really work for you."
- a priest in the confessional told you, "You're not gay. You're a beloved child of God." (The lesson here is that those are two opposite things.)

> My pastor was the first person in my life to accuse me of being gay and to label me as gay and to get me to verbally admit that I was gay. Four years later, he would drag me into a meeting and accuse me of using unbiblical labels to describe myself.
> –Bridget Eileen Rivera, @TravelingNun

- the shame you feel knowing that you have both Grindr and the Mass Times app on your phone makes you check Grindr more and Mass Times less.
- you get panic attacks on the way to church, but you go anyway; you feel free and safe at Pride parades and wonder if that should make you ashamed.

- you've cursed out Jesus and then told him, "I will always love you. But I know you don't want me."[7]
- you've wondered if you'll go to hell if you say, "I love you."

Complicity

It's hard to confront these painful stories because it's hard to remember how much we've suffered; it's hard to admit that we were scared, powerless, humiliated, that we believed the lies others told us about our own experiences.

But for some of us it's also hard to confront these stories because they force us to remember the ways in which we ourselves have participated in Christian homophobia. Hearing others' stories has forced me to reckon with some of my own past actions: the way I, too, contributed to a Christian culture that destroyed gay people's faith.

And so I owe gay communities an apology for the ways in which my own actions have contributed to homophobia in the churches. There are probably a lot of those ways—everyone is more complicit than we think we are—but specifically in the 2000s I did a lot of writing and speaking against gay marriage, and I did clerical work for one of the major groups opposing it.[8] I don't intend to rehash those arguments, and I also don't intend to recant them; I still think our country should have found a better solution to the real needs of gay couples than reshaping an institution designed to guide heterosexual eros away from its immense potential for chaos and destruction.

But I do want to apologize for my willful ignorance of the conditions in which all opposition to gay marriage took place. While I was giving unsuccessful speeches about the unique risks and responsibilities of heterosexual intercourse, kids growing up in Christian churches were hearing, over and over, that the gays were destroying America. While I was struggling to articulate possibilities for supporting nonmarital kinship, gay kids were hearing that God didn't want them to have a future of love and care. I was arguing that *the only* path our laws and culture actually, currently provided for adult kinship and love should be barred to gay people.

I recently spoke with a young woman who was attending a suburban Texas high school in 2003, when Massachusetts legalized gay marriage. She told me that every single day—literally—her classmates said that gay people were going to hell. She had been raised in a completely secular home, but she started reading the Bible in order to argue with Christians. She was able, in spite of the counterwitness by the Christians all around her, to see the pattern in the Bible of God's protection and love of oppressed people. She began to see the Bible as a text of liberation, one meant for her even though she wasn't straight. So she started going to a fundamentalist church, despite knowing nobody there would accept her if they knew she was interested in women. I don't know how she was able to see through the lies of Christian homophobia. Was it strength of will or mental toughness? Was it the grace of God? Whatever it was, she kept going to church, she survived to adulthood, she came out of the closet, and that's how I met her. But there were thousands upon thousands like her whom I will never meet because they dropped out of church—or out of life.

I don't know if recognizing that reality would have changed my beliefs about gay marriage as a civil institution. It hasn't yet. But I do know that acknowledging this reality would have—and should have—changed how I spent my time and energy. I aided in the destruction of a generation's faith that God was on their side.

Asking forgiveness should always be a way of humbling one-self and putting power in other people's hands, rather than a way of imposing a duty on others. In that spirit I ask forgiveness from (especially, but not only) LGBT people. You don't owe it to me—you don't owe me anything, as I hope is obvious. And the people who were most damaged in those years are the ones for whom forgiveness would be most painful. But I think it's my responsibility to ask for it. I'm sorry.

Let's return to the drinking game. After all, we skipped some of the basic items. Remember, everything that follows has happened to real gay people who were trying to follow their church's sexual ethic.

Take a drink if . . .

- you lost a job or ministry position because you came out, or were outed by others. *Drain your drink* if you were told that you weren't a good fit for the position because your sexuality made you a threat to children.
- you aren't sure if you should drink for the previous item. Everybody said that your orientation was no problem, but then there was a *long* delay before you heard back from them that "something came up" and they were rescinding the job offer, and you remember how their faces looked when you said "gay." When this kind of thing happens more than once, not with the same details but the same general outline, you start to feel as if you're in a horror movie where everybody you know and trust *might* be a shape-shifting alien—or maybe you're just paranoid, and you can't even trust yourself.
- you were thrown out of your home because you came out, or were outed by others.

> **Kelley Cutler, a Catholic advocate on home-lessness, says: I have seen many youth who confided their sexual identity to their parents as they were just coming to terms with it themselves. Let me be clear that I**

am speaking about their sexual identity, not sexual behavior. Revealing their sexual identity resulted in them being kicked out of their home. I've seen many LGBT youth fresh on the street, who were virgins. I have seen many of these youth quickly fall into survival sex as a means to get housing, food, and money. I have seen many of these youth become addicted to drugs as a way to cope with the horror they are experiencing. I have seen many of these youth infected with HIV. I have seen many of these youth die. So I take this very seriously.

I'm not suggesting a LGBT youth should not go to their parents or priest. In fact, there are many priests I know who I would encourage an LGBT person to reach out to. What I am saying is that they need to put a lot of consideration into identifying if the person is safe for them to reach out to because the consequences can be dire. My hope is that the Church will explore more ways they can be a safe place for these youth.[9]

- you weren't thrown out of your house, because your parents tried to confine you to it. They took away your phone, and your computer if you had one. They only let you leave the house to go to school and church (and meetings with the Christian therapist who promised you confidentiality, then told your parents everything you said to her). They took your door off its hinges. You always thought this was such extreme behavior that nobody else could have experienced it, so you never bothered to mention it; decades later you discovered that scores of other gay teens were treated the same way.[10]

- when you came out of the closet, Christians gossiped about you and started avoiding your family. (By the way, like many of these items, this was still an injustice even if you also rejected the Christian sexual ethic.)

- you confided in someone about having experienced sexual abuse, and they told you, "Oh, that must be why you're gay."

- you haven't actually been abused but your counselor, pastor, or therapist assumed that you have, because you're gay. *Extra drink* if they tried to convince you that you were just repressing the memories.

- you confided in someone about having been in an abusive same-sex relationship as an adult, and they told you, "Well, I don't know what you expect from a sinful relationship."[11]

- you wondered if maybe that was right, since part of the reason your relationship turned abusive (on your side, or your partner's side, or both) was because you two were closeted and had nobody to talk to about your problems.[12] A relationship that secretly turned sexual then secretly turned jealous or obsessive and then, still secretly, turned violent. You had nobody to tell you which specific behaviors were selfish, manipulative, or cruel—all gay relationships were treated as an undifferentiated mass of sin.

- and then, when you got out of that awful relationship and were confused, guilt-ridden, and mourning, you had nobody to talk to about that either.

- you had no guidance at church, at home, or at school, so the only place you could learn what it meant to be gay was from porn. Or the sketchy guys you met through the Internet. Or the rapists you met through the Internet. Or, if you were lucky, terrible fanfiction called things like "Draco Potter-Malfoy and the Bedchamber of Secrets."

- you were punished by your Christian college because you hugged a dude. Like, not your boyfriend, even, just a guy friend. And then straight Christians told *you* to stop defining yourself by your sexuality!
- you've received spiritual counsel or therapy that assumed that chastity was your biggest struggle and same-sex attraction was the center of your spiritual life. (And then straight Christians told you to stop defining yourself by your sexuality.)
- other people assumed you were having sex with your best friend / housemate / second cousin once removed, and then blamed you for "giving scandal" by making them think about all the hot gay sex you weren't actually having.
- as soon as they found out you're gay, your pastor or other spiritual authority started to watch your friendships like the Stasi. If you had one same-sex friendship that did turn out badly (enmeshed, toxic, codependent—people have a lot of different terms they use), these mentors redoubled their suspicion of *all* your same-sex friendships. They advised you to keep away from anybody of the same sex who seemed to like you too much. They were shocked when this led you to bitterness, despair, or rejection of the Christian sexual ethic.

(I know these last four are basically all the same item, but it's ridiculous how everything I do is viewed as inherently sexual as soon as people find out I'm gay. It's as if gay people are an alien species from some *Star Trek*–themed porno, whose every limb is a sex organ.)

- your emotional openness and vulnerability with same-sex friends were called "neediness," "being enmeshed," or "codependence." Your traumatized guardedness and inability to trust were treated as evidence of spiritual maturity.
- you've been assaulted, threatened, or verbally harassed because you "look gay" or were being suspiciously intimate with someone of the same sex.

- your dad threatened to beat you up for being gay. Or really did it.
- your suicide attempt was the only thing that could finally make you admit you were gay.

Secular or progressive communities can provide their own items for this drinking game. You'll notice that these next ones are a lot less violent than some of the ones above, although over time they can also wear down a person's self-respect and trust in God and other people.

So hey, take a drink if . . .

- you've been called "self-hating" because of your faith, by people who think they're doing you a favor. "Poor thing, you have Stockholm Syndrome." "You think you can get them to treat you better by being celibate, but they still hate you. Sad!" (If they really believe we're being abused, it's sort of awful that they respond with judgmental pity, you know?)
- you've been told that your deepest friendships—forms of love that shape your life and may have saved it—are "just friendship," "not *real* love," or otherwise inferior to sexual relationships.
- you've shared some of your deepest and most harrowing spiritual experiences—the places where you've experienced God's mercy in the teeth of despair and shame—and the person you were talking to acted like you were crazy or foolish for making such a big deal about a little thing like being gay.
- you've taken your sins of lust to the confessional for forgiveness and reconciliation and been told that they're not really sins; or you were told, "It sounds like you really need to find a good boyfriend." Or girlfriend, for the ladies, although for some reason I've only heard of priests saying this stuff to men.
- you've been asked, in that way that's more like being told, "Why don't you just switch churches?" (Have you tried turning your conscience off and then turning it on again?) It's especially

helpful when the person asking you this question is your therapist. Really builds trust.

- you've been told, "Oh, I get it, you're asexual." I, uh, am not asexual, as literally all of my confessors know. Most people who accept celibacy for the sake of the kingdom of God aren't. It isn't that we find sex boring; it's that we believe God is asking us to sacrifice its pleasures for a joy immeasurably greater.

I think we need another break to sober up. So go ahead, take a drink if . . .

- you have *ever* heard a homily offering a vision for gay people's future in the Church, not counting progressive homilies about the good of gay marriage.
- your Christian school or youth group *ever* offered sex-ed or guidance in chastity that not only acknowledged that some Christian kids are gay, but welcomed them and offered realistic, hopeful guidance for their futures.
- your school or local public library had even one book by a gay person who shares your convictions on sexuality. (No disrespect to Oscar Wilde, who died in the arms of Holy Mother Church, but for the purposes of this specific item he doesn't count.)
- you *ever*, growing up, saw a character on TV or in a movie who shared both your sexuality and your faith. A character who wasn't trying to be "ex-gay," who wasn't suicidal or closeted, who didn't have a heartwarming realization that the Church was wrong all along and gay sex is A-OK with Jesus—but who had a life, a faith, and a future you might want.

LOL, I *know* none of you all drank that time.

- nobody at your church has ever acted suspicious or weird because you're a butch lady or a flaming dude.
- your church welcomes your covenant friend,[13] celibate partner, or "sister/brother in Christ" as a member of your family and

offers you two the exact same hospitality and care they would offer a married couple, with no wincing distance or creepy gossip. *Extra drink* if you didn't have to try like fifty churches before finding this one—and by the way, where do you live? *Extra drink* if your mom rejoiced when you introduced your partner. (And call your mother!)

- when you made mistakes, including sinful and hurtful mistakes, while trying to lead a life almost totally without guidance—a kind of life for which you had vanishingly few models, if any—your pastors and counselors treated your failures with compassion and understanding, instead of trying to make you see how stupid you'd been to try in the first place.
- your church, before it tried to teach or rebuke gay people, sought to defend them.

So here we are, gazing out over the wreckage of our drinking game: a tabletop and floor covered with sticky empty Solo cups, in ranks like tombstones. Each item I've listed above represents thousands upon thousands of lives distorted by shame and despair, by false conceptions of God. Each item represents thousands upon thousands of churches where the best that gay people can hope for is total silence about our futures.

It doesn't have to be this way. In the rest of this book I'll point to resources in scripture and Christian practice that can restore our trust in a God who loves us, who shepherds us with infinite mercy and tenderness.

We can start in the place where gay people often feel the most anxiety and fear—and where our longings are treated with the greatest suspicion. What does the Bible say about same-sex love? You have been taught, at most, only half of the story.

Part II

WHAT IF "BAD THINGS" ARE ... GOOD?

two

ORDER IN
SAME-SEX LOVE

In 1945, two men met in wartime London. Dunstan Thompson was
a poet and socialite: a Harvard dropout raised Catholic in Maryland, now serving in the U.S. Army. Philip Trower was a British
intelligence officer. Thompson was stationed in England, where
the two men crossed paths—the beginning of a love that would
last through both their lifetimes, reshape Thompson's poetry, and
help reconcile their souls to God.

At first they lived like normal homosexuals of their time. They
settled in a town that rejoices in the name "Cley next the Sea."
Trower, inspired by Thompson's example, became a journalist, and
Thompson published poetry, fiction, and travel writing to, at best,
modest success.

The changes love was working in their lives began to show
in Thompson's poetry first. His previous poems were turbulent,
guilt-wracked, feverish tales of men degraded and even destroyed
by lovers who were part angel, part demon:

> The red-haired robber in the ravished bed
> Is doomsday driven, and averts his head,
> Turning to spurn the spoiled subjected body,
> That, lately lying altar for his ardor,
> Uncandled, scandalizes him, afraid he
> Has lost his lifetime in a moment's murder:
> He is the sinner who is saint instead:
> The dark night makes him wish that he were dead.[1]

Dana Gioia, whose 2015 essay "Two Poets Named Dunstan Thompson" introduced me to this fascinating poet, writes:

> The speaker compulsively bares his suffering and con-
> fusion to the reader—his hunger for male love, sexual
> guilt, painful romantic rejection, fear of death. Today
> these may be standard topics in undergraduate writing
> workshops, but in the wartime years these were not
> easy confessions to make, especially for an American
> in uniform. Thompson's self-exposure came at the risk
> of public shame and potential persecution—particularly
> the admission of homosexual affairs with fellow ser-
> vicemen, which not only broke the law but also violated
> strict social codes of silence. "No tears in the writer,"
> Robert Frost claimed, "no tears in the reader."[2]

Thompson's poetic persona at this time, Gioia writes, was inflamed with "erotic ardor and existential panic."

But in the aftermath of war, under the influences of country life and domestic happiness, Thompson's poetry grew calm. He shifted from romantic, urgent, confessional poetry to classical themes handled elegantly. He began to experiment with form rather than sticking to a percussive iambic, that meter which thuds, inescap-ably, like a hangover headache or a fearful heart. Now he can write lines like, "The end of love is that the heart is still. . . . Here I have found, as after thunder showers, / The friend my childhood prom-ised me. . . ."[3]

Now Thompson was openly grateful and unashamedly at home. He no longer believed himself incapable of holding love and responsibility together in one hand. He was cherished and he cherished someone else.

And in this atmosphere of sudden calm he became again, for the first time since Harvard, a practicing Catholic. It's impossible to say what prompts conversion, other than the Holy Spirit working secretly within us. Thompson had been slowly picking up bits and pieces of his discarded faith: the Rosary, a quick stop in a church to hear a homily, even a trip to Rome in 1950 to attend Pope Pius XII's proclamation of the dogma of the Assumption of the Virgin Mary. He and Trower bicycled together to witness a pilgrimage to the shrine of Our Lady of Walsingham, not far from where they lived—and when the procession with the Eucharist passed by them, Thompson fell to his knees and crossed himself.[4]

And then in 1952, after seven years with Trower, Thompson told his partner that he planned to make his Confession and return to practicing his faith. Decades later, Trower recalled: "If he took this step, Dunstan explained before he set out for London, the nature of our relationship would have to change. We should have to live chastely. It is also possible he would be told we could no longer live together. Was I prepared for this. I said Yes."[5]

This terse surrender conceals Trower's own religious journey; according to one friend, he'd already had doubts about the morality of their sexual relationship.[6] Whatever complex mix of emotions of sacrifice or liberation he experienced with Thompson's return to faith, six months later Trower, raised Anglican, joined his partner in the Catholic Church. The two men did, in fact, begin to live chastely. But they didn't stop loving each other. Nor did they live separately:

> The two men also made the bold move to ask for ecclesiastical permission to live together as a celibate couple, which, *mirabile dictu*, was granted. (Their spiritual advisor wisely felt that they would live their faith more successfully together than apart.) Although their platonic lifestyle has been criticized by some gay commentators (and their ecclesiastical license has astonished some Catholic ones), the couple's decision evidently worked. The two men spent the rest of their life together as a loving, contented, and very Catholic couple—a happiness attested to over the years by many visitors, both gay and straight.[7]

The poetry Thompson wrote from within his Catholic faith has not only a different cadence but a different symbolic vocabulary. In the early poems love is a hall of mirrors, a garden of sterile flowers, a predator, an enemy. The poems written after his return to faith can be playful (one describes saints so holy that even the fleas in their hair are praying!), but their most common emotional note is a trusting relief. Poems like "Magdalen" and "Halfway House" suggest that we become most ourselves when we reject our self-will, when we stop trying to have things our own way. Heaven is friendship—one of the few terms that recurs as frequently in the later poems as in the earlier ones, but spoken now with delight and not ambivalence or fear. Heaven is home, love, and the happiness of being one's true self.

Thompson's earthly domestic love seems to have offered him a foretaste of this happiness. Thompson and Trower lived in peace, welcoming a parade of visitors including gay couples and Catholic bishops, frequently acting as altar servers and celebrating happy hour every day, until Thompson's death in 1975.[8] Trower promoted Thompson's literary legacy and followed him into the arms of their Savior in 2019. A tribute from Thompson to Trower includes this utterly lovely statement:

> I owe my heart
> Unfettered and my soul at rest.
> To you, who offer more than all my art
> Can match.[9]

In "Two Poets Named Dunstan Thompson" (the two poets are the same man) Gioia makes the acute comments,

> A common assumption about Thompson's career is that he changed from a glorious gay pagan celebrating the world, the flesh, and the devil to a pious Catholic contemplating eternity, the soul, and salvation. Such a neat dichotomy makes it easy to generalize about the poetry. The problem is that a careful study of the work itself

does not support the theory that Thompson changed (in Edward Field's pithy but inaccurate formula) "from brilliant bad boy to repentant sinner." . . .

The early poetry is as deeply and explicitly theological as the later work. What mostly differs is the speaker's perceived relationship toward grace and redemption. Edward Field's formula is exactly backwards: only in Thompson's early work does the persona of the guilt-ridden sinner appear.[10]

In the poems of the "first Dunstan Thompson," the desperate and lost romantic, Catholicism emerges in lines about "[t]he garbage gift of faith, slag-heap of hope."[11] The "second Dunstan Thompson," on the other hand, writes with confidence, calm, and the hope of the rescued survivor on a life raft floating toward that "paradise" where "cats are kind to mice," where we'll find "the road at an end / And each one a friend."[12]

The second Dunstan Thompson is the same person as the first one, but now liberated and given peace by Christ—and by the other man he loved.

Biblical Love

One way the Catholic Church speaks about homosexuality is by using the phrase "objectively disordered." This phrase appears in the 2000 *Catechism* to describe a "homosexual . . . inclination."[13] And it has done a lot of damage—but if we look at this phrase with eyes less conditioned by our culture, we may be able to see it as a beacon of hope.

There are two main reasons the idea of homosexuality as "objective disorder" has made it hard for gay people to imagine a future in the Church. The first is that we are used to hearing the term "disorder" applied to medical conditions. I have a bleeding disorder, for example, which makes surgery more risky and nosebleeds more annoying. We especially use the term "disorder" in psychiatric contexts: eating disorder, attention deficit disorder, post-traumatic stress disorder. And I don't need to rehearse here the harrowing history of treating homosexuality as a psychiatric illness. Saying that homosexuality is a "disorder" evokes more than a century of attempted "cures," from chemical castration to forcing gay men to watch pornography.[14] Men and women were locked into mental hospitals for being gay.[15]

One might respond, "Yes, this might be an unfortunate rhetorical choice in our current culture. But Catholic teaching has a rich understanding of 'order,' in which it means, essentially, harmony with one's nature as a human being. All sins are disordered in this understanding, because they take us out of our place in the order of creation."

The second problem, then, is not merely about the coincidence of a word appearing in both theology and psychiatric history. (Assuming that it is a coincidence, and not a capitulation to secular medical accounts of homosexuality as curable mental illness.) The second and much deeper problem lies in the way Christians have expected people's longings to become *ordered*. What is the harmony we hope to bring forth from the cacophony of our desires? What is our hymn of praise to God—a hymn enacted with our bodies?

Almost exclusively, since the nineteenth century and the emergence of "homosexuality" as a condition (versus "sodomy" as an action),[16] Christians have assumed that homosexuality becomes ordered when it becomes heterosexuality. The goal has been to make homosexuals dissolve into the heterosexual majority. It is our duty to learn to live like them, we're told; they have nothing to learn from us.

As it happens, the project of shoving homosexuals into the devil's own Play-Doh Fun Factory and squeezing them out in perfectly straight lines has been a colossal failure. All the manliness retreats, all the talk therapy, all the slow-release synthetic estrogen injections[17] and electroshock, left the large majority of people still

implacably, indomitably homosexual. Often traumatized, sometimes married with kids—or at least divorced with kids—but still
gay. The 2013 closure of Exodus International, the largest "ex-gay"
ministry in the world, marked the beginning of the end for the
"cure" approach to homosexuality.[18]
We are so lucky that these cures failed.

In the wake of the failure of the cures, we have been forced to
ask whether there is any other way in which same-sex desires can
become ordered. And we do find an alternative path—in fact, we
find this path winding throughout scripture, utterly ignored and
yet necessary for Christians of many sexual orientations. What
if, instead of trying to switch our sexual desires from homo- to
hetero-, we tried to express our gay desires chastely? What if we
sought to honor and express our longings to love, share our lives
with, commit to, cherish, serve, make a home with, and become
family to someone of the same sex?

The Bible uses both opposite-sex *and same-sex* love to teach
us what love truly means. Both kinds of love are used as images
of the love God has for his people and for our individual souls;
both kinds of love are used as models for how we should live in
relationship to God.

These two kinds of love are not interchangeable. They have
different structures, different expressions. Whenever the Bible uses
sexual love to teach us about the mutual love of God and human-
kind, it's always the love of one man and one woman, as in the Song
of Songs or Ephesians 5. Whenever the Bible uses same-sex love to
teach us about God's love for us and ours for him, it is nonsexual
and nonmarital love. (Scripture, unlike contemporary Western culture, does not use the terms "intimacy," "devotion," "commitment,"
or even "love" itself as mere euphemisms for sex.) But in scripture,
same-sex and opposite-sex love are equally intimate, equally sac-
rificial—equally real and holy.

In what follows, I'll look at three of scripture's love stories—
David and Jonathan, Ruth and Naomi, and Jesus and John. These

pairs' experience of same-sex love is not marginal to their own lives; it isn't a kind of accessory that is nice to have but nothing compared to the *real* love of marriage and children. It is life-shaping in its emotional power. Nor is their experience of same-sex love abstract or intellectual. It's visceral and practical.

Nor are these loves marginal to the story the Bible is telling. If we imagine scripture as a human body, these same-sex loves aren't the big toe or even the right thumb, nice to have but okay to lose. They are all part of the very spine of scripture: the story of God's lasting covenant with his children and our rescue by Jesus, our Savior. Our reluctance to explore these images of love, therefore, has distorted our emotional lives, our practical ability to form families and communities, and our understanding of Jesus' mission. Rediscovering these stories is among the greatest of the many gifts gay Christians can give to our churches.

David and Jonathan

We first see devoted same-sex love in the lives of David and Jonathan. They meet in the first book of Samuel, just after David slays Goliath. Jonathan is the son and heir apparent of King Saul, but David is the one God has chosen to be king. We might expect Jonathan to resent David, or at least be suspicious of him as a potential rival.

But instead, Jonathan immediately gives his heart to David: "By the time David finished speaking with Saul, Jonathan's life became bound up with David's life; he loved him as his very self. . . Jonathan and David made a covenant, because Jonathan loved him as his very self" (1 Sm 18:1, 3).

David offers an unforgettable tribute to Jonathan after the latter's death:

> I grieve for you, Jonathan my brother!
> Most dear have you been to me;

More wondrous your love to me
than the love of women. (2 Sm 1:26)

This lament is double-edged given that King David, perhaps
the Bible's most notorious heterosexual, rarely loved women well.
I don't know that Michal or Bathsheba would have thrilled to hear
this paean to the faithful love David received from his fallen friend.
Nonetheless, three things about David and Jonathan's love
stand out to a contemporary reader. One is simply the emotional
intensity of it, obvious from their very first meeting all the way to
David's anguish after Jonathan's death.

Another is the fact that the two men used symbolic actions
familiar to their culture in order to solemnify their friendship.
Jonathan gives David his armor in 1 Samuel 18:4. To the readers of
the Bible, this can foreshadow the fact that David will be the next
king, and it symbolizes Jonathan's acceptance that David, and not
he, will rule Israel. But this exchange also serves to formalize the
bond between the two men. Ron Belgau, in his essay "Love, Covenant, and Friendship" (which heavily influenced my understanding
of these issues), compares Jonathan and David here to Glaucus and
Diomedes exchanging armor in the *Iliad*.[19] This ritual makes their
friendship more than an emotional tie; it imposes obligations that
they must honor even if their feelings shift or fade. It unites their
families: Jonathan makes reference to this kinship in 1 Samuel
20:14–17 and again in 1 Samuel 20:42. Their friendship is truly a
covenant, an image of the covenant between God and his people.

And the third startling aspect of David and Jonathan's friendship is how clearly Jonathan's role foreshadows Jesus' challenge,
"No one has greater love than this, to lay down one's life for one's
friends" (Jn 15:13—how fitting that it's in John!). For love of God
and David, Jonathan surrenders his status as the next king, his
relationship with his father, and his physical safety. He obeys both
God and David, God's chosen king: "Jonathan then said to David,
'I will do whatever you say'" (1 Sm 20:4). His friendship with David
requires both obedience and sacrifice and is beautified by these acts.

We know that David in his kingship prefigures the divine lord-ship of his lineal descendant Jesus. The first reading for the Solemnity of Our Lord Jesus Christ, King of the Universe, is 2 Samuel 5:1–3, in which the tribes of Israel pledge to obey David and David is anointed king. And Jonathan's obedience to David expresses this prefigurative meaning well.

But as we explore the love of David and Jonathan, we see that Jonathan also—in an especially striking and mystical way—prefigures Jesus' lordship. Jonathan lays down his kingship *so that David can become king*, in a startling foreshadowing of the way Jesus lays down his life for us and offers us the "divinization" that Christians believe God has promised us: we will become what St. Thomas Aquinas called "partakers of the divine nature." St. Athanasius even more shockingly expressed this idea when he wrote, "To make human beings gods, he was made man who was God."[20] Jonathan's friendship teaches us about both Jesus' love for us and our friendship with Jesus.[21]

Jesus, though he had the rights and power of a king, took on our lowliness and weakness (see Philippians 2:6–8). He who was one in being with the Father was brought to the depths of crying out, "My God, my God, why have you forsaken me?" As far as risking his physical safety was concerned, he gave his body to be tortured and killed so that by his stripes we might be healed, and he comes to us every day in his most helpless form, to be broken for us in the Eucharist. And he did all of this to make us like himself. Jesus' love for us is wonderful, surpassing *even* the love of Jonathan.

Ruth and Naomi

I first heard the promises of Ruth to Naomi in a lesbian folk song. The singer infused each word with longing and trust as she sang a variant of the words we hear in the Mass readings: "Wherever you go, I will go. . . . Your people shall be my people." Her voice soared as she reached the final promise: "and your God, my God" (Ru 1:16).[22]

These verses are sometimes used at lesbian weddings as the vows of the couple.[23] That might seem like a strange choice. After all, Ruth and Naomi are not fancy-free single women who met at a Moab book club or bar. Ruth was Naomi's daughter-in-law. She makes these promises because out of all Naomi's daughters-in-law, she alone—whose husband has died, who could have left Naomi behind—chooses instead to make her life with her mother-in-law.

Regardless of your views on gay marriage, you'd have to be a pretty committed sexual progressive to suggest that it's a good idea to marry your mother-in-law. And yet it makes sense that Ruth's promises would be attractive to contemporary gay women. First of all, it's an expression of love between two women. Ruth chooses Naomi; her allegiance to Naomi's God is the fruit of her commitment to a woman who loves God. The possibility that God might not reject your love of another woman, but could even use it to bring you closer to him, is attractive to many religious lesbians—including those with a traditional sexual ethic.

The second aspect of Ruth's promises that should stand out to us is how clearly they speak to practical challenges we face in what might be called the postmodern economy. As I talk to more and more people who are trying to renew the historic Christian traditions of covenant friendship,[24] one problem that comes up again and again is, "What happens if I move away?" *Who will go with me, no matter where I go in life?* It's good to find a friend who is like a home for you—but when you leave that home, will you be simply homeless again? Or will your friend leave you behind, seeking work or a better place to raise a family? Will you start off talking to each other frequently on Skype or instant messages, but slowly find it harder and harder to find the time, especially since the face or text on the screen never offers the kind of lived-in love you used to know when you guys lived together? Will you go back to coming home to an empty apartment, with no one to take care of and no one who knows how you really live?

I'm working on this book during massive lockdowns and stay-at-home orders to prevent the spread of Covid-19. Here in DC, we've been told not to take public transportation unless our trip is "essential." I have a friend in Bethesda, Maryland, maybe a twenty-minute drive away, and it feels as if she's on the other side of the country. I'm staying with my parents temporarily, but if I were in my own apartment, walking here to see them would take me about two hours. And so I'm reminded quite forcefully of what it means to have someone who loves and cares for you *in your home*, sharing your life on a day-to-day basis. The question "Will anyone go with me wherever I go?" is also the question "Will I only be quarantined *away from,* or will I also be quarantined *with?*"

Pledging to share your life with someone and to go with her wherever she goes is nowadays almost exclusively reserved for romantic relationships. So Christians who think it very unlikely that they will end up married fear a future of temporary ties, sharing life's yoke only to a limited extent and never with someone who will stay with you no matter what. It can start to seem as if you're practicing "social distancing" from your own heart.

The book of Ruth speaks to these contemporary needs and fears. And it speaks in the same terms used by centuries of Christian friendship pairs. Ruth's promises mirror, in striking specificity, the promises made by pairs of same-sex friends in medieval and early modern societies. I wrote at length in *Gay and Catholic* about these friendships adorned with vows of care and permanence,[25] so I won't belabor the point here, except to note what I didn't notice back then: their parallel to Ruth's promises to Naomi. Friends could pledge to share "a common purse and a common table," meaning that they would live together and merge their households' finances ("Wherever you go, I will go"). They became members of one another's family, pledging to care for the friend's children if anything happened to him ("Your people shall be my people").[26] And they sometimes sealed these promises in the eyes of God by making them on the church steps or by hearing Mass together, exchanging the kiss of peace and receiving the Eucharist together; more often, they would stand as godfather to one another's children ("and your God, my God").[27]

Now look at these same pledges from the perspective of a contemporary believer—especially a gay Christian. "Wherever you go, I will go": I will stay with you. If we move, we will move together; we will make our home together and become home to each other. "Your people shall be my people": You are my family and I am your family. If your own family rejects you, or rejects us and won't acknowledge my role in your life, even so, you will have me and my kin for your kin. "And your God, my God": I will support you in your faith. I know the challenges you've faced, how hard it has been for you to trust God in a church that often doesn't seem to want you. I will help you to love Jesus, and by loving each other, we will learn to love him.

Ruth is one of a handful of women who appear in Matthew's genealogy of Jesus (see Matthew 1:5). Ruth the Moabite met Boaz, and so became one of the foremothers of the Savior, because she loved Naomi. Ruth, through her promises to Naomi, becomes one of the most prominent non-Hebrew women woven into the Hebrew Bible's story of the people of Israel; so her life foreshadows the way the Gentiles will be "grafted in" (Rom 11:17) to the Hebrew people. And so love between women is woven into salvation history.

And speaking of Jesus, our Savior . . . wait, no, before we look at same-sex love in the life of our Lord, let's first address one question you may be asking.

Who Are These Stories of Same-Sex Love For?

I rhapsodize about same-sex love in scripture and in Christian history because the love of women has shaped my own life, including my spiritual life. I wrote about this at length in *Gay and Catholic* so I won't rehash, but yes, these stories are important to me in part

because as a lesbian I've sought ways to love women in harmony
with the Catholic Church.

Does that mean these are "gay stories"? Is covenant friendship, or a "celibate partnership,"[28] the solution to gay Christians'
problem?

There are some serious reasons to answer, "LOL, no." I'll begin
with the reasons most relevant to actual queer people (because if
this book doesn't keep the margins at the center, who will?), and
then move on to the reason most relevant to our heterosexual
brethren.

First of all, I would hate for us to set up a different idol to
replace the idolatry of marriage. American culture, perhaps especially in the churches, already treats marriage as the "capstone"[29] of
a life: something you get to do only once you've attained emotional
and financial stability. We too often think of marriage almost like
a Good Housekeeping Seal of Approval on your life. Marriage and
parenting are *the* forms of love we know and honor. As the percent-
age of married people drops,[30] we have not seen a rise in celibacy
(i.e., unmarried life as a haven for fruitful service of God). We just
have a lot more people who feel that they've failed to marry.

And overemphasizing covenant friendship as a life path for
gay Christians, or making it seem like the best or normative life
path for us, risks creating an abstract, sexless "ideal gay Christian,"
a plaster saint who finds all her gayness easily fulfilled in chaste
friendship. Chastity is a sacrifice for most Christians. In the ex-gay
era, Christians treated gay people as a problem and tried to solve
us by making us straight and marrying us off. I do not want to
replicate this dehumanizing error by treating covenant friendship
as the solution to the "problem" of gay people. Nor do I want to
pretend that sexual desire can be easily or predictably sublimated
into friendship. Learning chaste celibacy in partnership is a long-
term process, a process of being worn down as rocks are reshaped
by crashing waves. It's more like learning how to be married than

deciding to get married. And it isn't something you earn; it's a gift you receive, from God and in the love and patience of your partner.

I have spoken to many gay Christians who desperately want a lifelong partnership with someone of the same sex. I write about covenant friendship because it is beautiful—and, crucially, because it is the principal way scripture uses same-sex love between adults to model God's love for us and ours for him.

But it is not the only way to live well as a gay Christian. It is not the way I'm living myself; my own closest friendships are not adorned with formal promises or vows, and yet they are beautiful and good. A covenant friendship or other formal partnership is not something God promises you, and in fact it's relatively rare. The numbers game offers one reason: there are relatively few gay people (fewer than you might think), and among those, very few practice the Christian sexual ethic (though *more* than you might think!) . . . and among *those*, not all will be open to a partnership . . . and among those, not all will be open to a partnership *with you*.

If you look for a way to pour yourself out in love, you will find it. If you look for a way to express your longings for same-sex love in harmony with your faith, you are fairly likely to find it. But new possibilities and new hopes bring with them new temptations. One temptation, as we rediscover scriptural forms of same-sex love, is that we will slot them too quickly into the place our society has given to marriage. We are not to cling to anything, even the beautiful things; we are not to demand them from God. I said last time around, "God doesn't only want from you the sacrifices you want to make," and that is still true when God asks you to sacrifice a dream of covenant friendship rather than a dream of gay marriage.

I know it's especially frustrating to learn that you *could* have so much more than you thought possible within God's will, and yet still not attain the life you long for. But God scatters love through our lives according to his will, not our expectations. We do best when we are willing to accept love wherever we find it: in friendships that aren't adorned with covenant promises, in service to

others, in community life; in teaching, art, care for your family of
origin or a "chosen family"; for some of us, in religious vows or
(even, rarely) marriage to someone of the opposite sex. Which of
these paths are open to us will be largely out of our control.

And turning now to our heterosexual brethren—I don't think
of covenant friendship as "the Christian form of gay love," because
it's not just for us! Same-sex love is part of the ecology of a flourishing Christian community. All the ways we can be bound to one
another, as godparents and "honorary aunties" and regular friends
and covenant friends, are open to everyone.

Often when I speak about devoted, promise-adorned same-sex
love, straight people will come up to me afterward and say this is
what they want for their own friendships. Many of them sense that
the lack of public honor for friendship and the lack of guidance
in forging lifelong friendships have harmed them as well. Many
of them love someone of the same sex, intensely and sacrificially,
and they want some way to pledge that they won't let their love
crumble under the pressure of parenting and other life changes.
Many of these are married people thinking of their gay friends,
or their straight unmarried friends. Knowing the blessings (and
obligations) of kinship that they've experienced in marriage, they
long to be family to unmarried friends.

The admittedly patchy historical evidence shows that covenants
and promises of friendship were often, perhaps usually, made by
people who also had a spouse. Vowed friendships linked households, as David's covenant with Jonathan links their houses and
makes Jonathan a part of David's children's family. David and Ruth
obviously marry others while maintaining the care and love that
prompted their vows of friendship. And the institution of godpar-
enting, where it continues to flourish, can weave a new adult into
the family.

A final consideration: As Christians we are not called to be
family solely to those we like and choose. Jesus rejects what we
might call an "overfocus on the family" when he asks, "Who is my

mother? Who are my brothers?" He answers his own question by gesturing toward his disciples and saying, "[W]hoever does the will of my heavenly Father is my brother, and sister, and mother" (Mt 12:46–50). In John 15:14 he defines friendship in a parallel way: "You are my friends if you do what I command you." Our understanding of family-making—whether in marriage or in covenant friendship, in godparenthood or in the more informal bonds of a "chosen family" of friends—must never allow these personal, exclusive loves to *crowd out* our membership in the Body of Christ and our responsibility toward our siblings in Christ.

Meg Baatz writes that God's "vision for family transcends any of our ideas founded upon human promise, biology, or fleshly need." She describes her life as a celibate gay woman living in community with a married couple, their children, and two other single people. "We all belong to the same small group and local church," she writes. "We share meals, prayers, parties, tears, and a dedication to resolving conflicts as they arise (and they do!). . . . [M]y favorite part is simple: at the end of the day, I have a beautiful family to come home to. Since entering into this domestic Christian community, burdens like loneliness, finances, temptation, an uncertain future, and even the Great Commission have become a lot lighter—and not just for me."[31]

So much love has been poured out, as service to those who need it most, by people who didn't know what else to do with their lives—who loved the neediest in part *because* they couldn't retreat into the haven of a marriage. Aaron Taylor writes:

> It does become problematic when the idea of the "chaste couple" is seen as a universal solution—a magic bullet that will solve the problem of gay loneliness. The risk is that over-emphasising chaste couplehood as a solution to loneliness becomes a way of telling gay Christians, "go away and find a partner so we don't have to deal with you, so we can pretend that the pain of your loneliness is not a burden we need to bear *as a community.*

There are many people in this world—gay, straight, and otherwise—for whom being one half of a couple is not a possible solution to loneliness. What about the elderly widow? What about the severely handicapped young man who needs 24-hour-a-day care and who will never marry? The radical inclusivity that we are called to if we wish to follow Jesus not only extends to such people, but has a *preferential option* for them.

Ultimately we will be judged not by our success at shoehorning everyone into modern models of couplehood, but by our success at fostering forms of community that go out to the peripheries and bring in those who are most marginalized, including those who do not and cannot enjoy the security marriage or couplehood brings.

The image of the Kingdom Jesus gives us is not an image of couples respectably making their way toward heaven, like the animals neatly marching into Noah's Ark two-by-two. Instead, the image of the Kingdom we get from reading the gospels is of a ragtag band of misfits, outcasts, and ragamuffins—the blind, the lame, the deaf, the poor, the drunkards, the whores, the sex addicts, the tax collectors, the queers, and the downright weird—leaning on one another as they zigzag their way toward the Promised Land. Likewise, when reading about the early Church, we see a sprawling network of friends bound together with a familial affection fostered through a shared focus on the joy of the gospel, and not the polite church of modern twenty-first century suburbia—a group of disconnected couples who happen to worship in the same place on Sunday morning.

Let's say "yes" to the possibility of chaste, gay couplehood as a vocation for some people. But let's also not forget that unless this "yes" is contextualized within openness to more radically inclusive forms of community, there is a danger that we are taking the easy and bourgeois path rather than the hard road to the Kingdom.[32]

I agree with everything Aaron says here, but what I hope gay people learn from the Christian history of same-sex love is simply that your desires do not exclude you from scripture's song of praise. And what I hope straight people see in this history is that honoring same-sex love can strengthen their own friendships, and thus their marriages (if they marry), families, and communities. As we all rediscover same-sex love, I hope it strengthens us to serve our communities, including the most difficult members—instead of prompting us to retreat into our private loves with a curt, "I've got mine, Jack."

Gay people need to know about the Bible's models of same-sex love because we have been told so often that our longing for intimacy and devoted commitment to someone of the same sex is inherently damaged or dirty. We've been made to fear our desires for intimacy. We've been made to feel as if our love of our friends is "too intense," immature, an imposition on the people we love. We've been made to feel that if we want to follow God's command, we have to start wanting that intimacy with someone of the opposite sex—and since that consistently doesn't happen, we find ourselves disobedient against our will.

This is a path to despair. It's a path to self-loathing. It's a path to viewing oneself as misbegotten from the start—not "wonderfully made" (Ps 139:14), but born incapable of obedience to God or real love of another person.

I've seen the way someone's face changes when she begins to accept that her longing to love another woman might be a lamp given her by God to light the path ahead. I've seen hope and relief wash over people when they realize that God is asking them to sacrifice sexual union, yes, but not the love they always knew played a role in their orientation. To see sex as the wrong expression of a love that has several right expressions—and is honored in scripture—offers far more hope than to see disordered sexual desire as proof that the longing for love is also disordered and must be straightened out. God didn't let your heart leap when you see someone you love, let a smile burst onto your face when she walks in the room, just to laugh at you like a middle-school bully and tell you your feelings are worthless. Rediscovering these models of same-sex love can change our relationship to scripture and our understanding of how God sees us.

So, yes, gay people need these models with an especial urgency, and we therefore have an obvious reason to seek them out and try to revive them.

It would be enough if these forms of love were only for us. But as we rediscover them, we offer them as gifts to all our churches.

Jesus and John

The third day belongeth to St. John,
Who was Christ's darling, dearer none.
   —a medieval carol for December 27,
      the Feast of St. John the Apostle

There are two people in the Gospel of John who are never referred to by name. Mary is always "the mother of Jesus"; John himself is always "the disciple whom Jesus loved." They are defined solely, insistently by their relationship to Jesus, as if they are person-shaped windows made transparent so the unconquerable Light can shine through.

There's something perversely showy about John's self-erasure. In *Infinite Jest*, David Foster Wallace creates a character so submissive to the 12-step ethic of anonymity that he becomes known as the Guy That Didn't Even Use His First Name.[33] Among a crowd of Don G.s and Joelle V.s, the Guy That Didn't Even Use His First Name can't help but stand out. But of course St. John the Beloved (as he's often called in our churches) was not trying to erase his own identity, but to point to the One who had reshaped it. The showiness of his insistence on anonymity shines a spotlight on the name he *does* use: the Name above all names. There is no definite record of how John's life ended, though most authorities agree that he did not receive the crown of martyrdom; unlike Peter, and unlike John's own brother James, he was not allowed to witness to Christ by his death. And yet in his writing he enacts a kind of martyrdom of his personal identity, crucifying his name so that it can bear witness to the Name.

Jesus uses "friendship" as one of the primary images by which we are to understand what it means to be his disciple. "No one has greater love than this," he says in John 15:13—and we might expect him to say that the greatest love is the love of a mother for her child, or a husband for his wife—but instead he says, "to lay down one's life for one's friends." He goes on to explain what his friendship demands, and what it offers: "You are my friends if you do what I command you. I no longer call you slaves, because a slave does not know what his master is doing. I have called you friends, because I have told you everything I have heard from my Father" (Jn 15:14–15).

In this sense Jesus' friends are countless men and women, including most of the people reading this book. But if we want to understand what God thinks of our longings for same-sex love and intimacy, we might take notice of the fact that he had an especially close and tender relationship with one disciple—the Disciple That Doesn't Even Use His First Name.

We see their intimacy most clearly at the Last Supper, and then at the foot of the Cross. At the Last Supper, John reclines at Jesus' side and leans against Jesus' breast to ask which of the disciples will betray him. Peter indicated that John should ask the question—perhaps he hesitated to ask it himself, unwilling to voice his own fear that he might not remain faithful. I doubt anyone thought that John might be the faithless one. So John's eyes turn upward trustingly to meet the eyes of his Lord. Because of his greater closeness to Jesus, he asks the question they all want to ask; and Jesus answers him.

Cardinal Robert Sarah compares John to "a faithful dog who takes his place at his master's feet."[34] And Cardinal Sarah points out, "This physical proximity is much more than bodily; we are talking about a spiritual graft and an intimate communion that allows Saint John to experience the same sentiments that Jesus does. The one whom Christ 'loved' is the Apostle who best described the unfathomable depths of the heart of the Son of God."[35]

John's gospel is famously mystical. It is John who tells us that Jesus is the eternal Word made flesh. He is both the Best Friend and the Light that shines in the darkness. Intimacy and awe are both raised to their height in this gospel, as if it were a microcosm of the mystery of the Incarnation.

At the Cross almost all the men have run away. Jesus' mother is there, along with other women disciples—and John. John's friendship with Jesus, which is perhaps our clearest model for our own friendship with him, does not shrink back from the Cross but stays with the Lord no matter what.

Jesus, though he is in agony and approaching death, makes sure to provide for Mary by giving her into John's care, making them kin to each other. "When Jesus saw his mother and the disciple there whom he loved, he said to his mother, 'Woman, behold your son.' Then he said to the disciple, 'Behold, your mother.' And from that hour the disciple took her into his home" (Jn 19:26–7).

The morning prayers for St. John's feast day include the prayer, "To the virgin John, Christ, dying on the Cross, entrusted his virgin mother."[36] This is an image of family-making within virginity, a kinship not diminished by sexual renunciation but forged within it. This is the gospel passage chosen for the recently instituted Feast of Mary, Mother of the Church. John, here, stands for every one of us who calls on Mary, our mother. In this passage, Mary becomes our mother because Jesus is our friend.

Friendship, in the gospels, is *at least* as intimate, committed, and life-shaping as marriage. Jesus' friendships are relationships with literally real people, as opposed to his union with his Bride the Church, which is a beautiful image (and one that played a role in my own conversion) conveying a truth, but only an image nonetheless. If marriage is the *most* real human relationship, the deepest and truest form of love between adults, why did Jesus himself not practice it? If same-sex love is an immature stage of development, to be grown out of as we learn to take on the real adult responsibilities of marriage and childrearing, why did our Lord live out his friendship with John so that its consequences lasted even after his death and resurrection?

In showing us the place Jesus held in John's heart, the gospels show us the place Jesus must hold in our own. And in showing us the place John held in Jesus' Sacred Heart, the gospels show us not only how he loves us but how we may love one another.

The Crisis of Love

There is often so much beauty, self-gift, and holiness in our own same-sex loves and in the same-sex loves of the people around us. Scripture is not silent about this beauty. These loves are not simply blank spaces, places where God turns his face away, aching absent limbs in the body of scripture. God in his Word and in the history of the Church offers us guidance on how to bring our disorderly loves into harmony with his will.

I know several gay Christians who have had the same experience: They were raised Christian; "good kids," trying to be obedient. Once they realized they were gay, they accepted this as "their cross" and did their best to cope with it, the way they do their best at everything in the spiritual life. Most of them tried to become straight, and after much anguish, they gave up trying and sought to find peace in their situation. They thought they were happy, and if you asked them if God loved them, they would have said, "Of course!"

Then one day they fell in love with another man, or another woman. And that person loved them back. They experienced, for the first time, being loved in a way where their sexual orientation wasn't a "cross" or a "challenge," not something to be tolerated or even merely accepted—where what had shamed them most was suddenly an attractive feature.

And it was this experience of love that prompted the religious crisis they'd managed to forestall until their late twenties or early thirties. At last they were forced to confront the fact that they had never believed that God loved them—at least not with the depth and honesty and delight of this other gay person's love. They had viewed themselves with disappointment and distaste and had striven anxiously to apologize to God, through their good behavior, for the crime of being gay.

Through anguish, prayer, courage; in the face of cruelty, indifference, and terrible advice; in service to their church and often to other gay people, they had moved, with painful steps, from total darkness into a kind of twilight that was all they knew of day. And now, in their very first experience of requited gay love, they stood in the sun.

Of course this experience reshaped their faith. How could it not? For some people this experience was terrifying; feeling themselves incapable of grappling with it, they withdrew from other people, sometimes turning to anonymous sex or other expressions of shame. For some, the experience of requited gay love was part of their journey out of the Church, or from a church that prohibited gay sex to one that performed gay marriages.

For others, the experience of requited gay love was tumultuous and even traumatic at first—the cracking of Arctic ice thickened by millennia of shame and self-rejection, a cataclysm within the soul—but it led to profound healing. It led them to reassess not what they believed about sex, but what they believed about God. These people have found themselves on the other side of the cataclysm still orthodox, but with a new character to their belief: an orthodoxy of trust in God's ardent and tender love, not an orthodoxy based on fear of sin or fear of disappointing God. They discovered how distant they were from God—how high a wall their upbringing and culture had built between gay people and the Lord. And they know now that God *wants* to break down that wall so they can cling to him.

This is a simplified narrative, of course. Many people go back and forth about their beliefs, as their long-held convictions meet, again and again, homophobia and silence in their churches. The more judgment and suspicion people encounter, the less likely they are to be able to see the Christian sexual ethic as a school of love and self-gift.

Christian rhetoric does great damage here. Christians often act as if we can't see real love in gay marriages. It's as if the sin, which is real, renders the love between the partners (and their love of God, if they are believers) unreal. We don't speak this way about other crucial religious differences; you rarely nowadays hear Catholics suggesting that Presbyterians are just incapable of loving God, or that the heresy of their Baptist neighbors renders Baptists' love of Jesus irrelevant or fake.

The individual gay Christian sees relationships where the partners sacrifice for each other, care for each other, and learn patience and humility. Then she hears these relationships always described solely in terms of sexual sin—by people who claim to speak for God. If you don't know love when you see it, why should we trust you to guide us to the God who is Love?

Dunstan Thompson and Philip Trower offer a better way of understanding the ordering of the soul. God brought peace to their chaotic loves. But he did it by stages; and he did not do it in the way their society would have led them to expect. Thompson's early promiscuity seems to have been (if we can judge by the violent, tormented tone of his poetry at that time) a kind of writhing in bondage. He was enslaved not only to sexual sin—not *primarily* to sexual sin. If I can go a little beyond what we really know, based on my friendships with gay men who grew up Christian and have had similar experiences with anonymous sex, I would suggest that what bound Thompson was the identification of pleasure and self-destruction.

Sexual pleasure can offer a brief escape to people who can't stand themselves. Anonymous sex is especially well-suited for this because you gain the other man's approval, you experience a certain real contact with another soul, and get a cocaine boost for your ego—but then he goes away, so you never have to reckon with the possibility that you are genuinely loved. Anonymous sex offers relief without change.

Happiness can't be used in this way. The peace and self-knowledge that come with years of service will always change you. Happiness is membership in a community that knows you in a way you can't be known otherwise, whether that community is a church ministry or a recovery group, a friendship or a marriage, a family or a monastery, the Catholic Worker or your tiny hometown—or the community of an individual soul and her God. Happiness is in the long haul. In our smaller, contingent human relationships we learn how to live toward happiness, and this slow education prepares us for the bliss of life with God.

It seems obvious that Thompson's early relationship with Trower—the love they shared before they became Catholic and chaste—was precisely a part of this education in happiness, which is also an education in order. Thompson's loves became ordered, and his life became peaceful, not because he rooted out his same-sex desires, but because he learned how to live them rightly.

I don't know to what extent Thompson or Trower continued to experience sexual temptation. Most of us are tempted in this way for most of our lives—that's why sex is so effective in humbling our pride. But learning to live friendship well includes learning to live friendship chastely, and many gay people have experienced greater peace in our celibacy precisely through deepening and committing ourselves more to our relationships with beloved people of the same sex.

Partnered celibacy, like the love of Thompson and Trower, is a way of life that our culture doesn't recognize at all. Unpartnered celibacy, by far the more common kind, is a way of life that our culture has trained us to see *solely* as a deprivation. Where does God meet us in any form of celibacy? What is its purpose, beyond "keeping people from doing bad sex things"? Can celibacy become a refuge where we experience God's tenderness, not a bitter and barren isolation?

That's the subject of the next chapter.

three

THE SECRET GARDEN

There's a painting by Francisco Ribalta showing a real event in the life of St. Bernard of Clairvaux.[1] St. Bernard, whose lyrical and longing sermons on the Song of Songs cast himself and his monks in the role of the bride wandering the city walls, here kneels in darkness, spotlit by the desert-white lighting of Spanish Counter-Reformation painting. In his white habit he embraces his beloved: Jesus, nearly naked, seated above him and bending down to gaze at him. St. Bernard's eyes are closed as he yields himself completely to Jesus.

This mystical encounter of the twelfth-century monastic reformer with Christ himself is described by the Jesuit historian Pedro de Ribadeneyra: "The Lord so cherished Saint Bernard that one day when the latter was kneeling before the Cross, the Crucified Christ stretched out his arm and lay it on him, embracing and stroking him most lovingly. Immersed in this ineffable gentleness and deep silence, he united with the Supreme Being in an extremely chaste embrace."[2]

Ribalta's painting, completed circa 1624–1627, is astonishingly intimate and tender. In the background are barely visible faces. They remind us of the other people surrounding this time-bending embrace: Bernard's monks, whose care must have been uppermost in his mind most of the time, and all those who witnessed Jesus' suffering on the Cross. But these faces fade into darkness. The clamor of care and witness gives way to the hush of the bridal chamber where Bernard's soul at last embraces her Lover, her Lord.

Jesus bleeds, yet his eyes and face are not agonized but calm. Bernard's head rests on Jesus' arm, and his face shows not only ecstasy but relief.

Bernard lived a life of political complexity and failure—he accepted responsibility for the failure of the Second Crusade, with which he had been closely identified. Pressed on all sides by controversies, schism, spiritual children, task after task, he must have been so grateful for every intimacy with Jesus: the one thing in his life he couldn't possibly take responsibility for.[3]

In this painting Ribalta shows a celibate whose whole life, all of his ascetic practice, and perhaps even especially his celibacy, was a yearning for this union with Christ. This moment is Bernard's foretaste of heaven, his glimpse of home on the long earthly journey. It is lyrical and physical. It is a portrait of what celibacy is primarily for: the tender embrace of Jesus. In this chapter I will explore what Christians have historically intended to do with celibacy, as well as how gay Christians' particular challenges and insights can guide churches in making celibacy a haven for communion with Christ.

In what follows I will do my best to represent Christian traditions accurately, but keep in mind that I am not a theologian; I mostly write movie reviews. And this chapter won't discuss *how* to have joy in celibacy. You probably know more about your own needs in that area than I do. Later chapters will address specific difficulties in gay Christian life, such as sexual sin, ambivalent faith, and suffering, which affect our ability to find joy in celibacy, but this chapter is solely about the purposes of celibacy: Why have Christians, since the Resurrection of the virgin Jesus, praised celibacy and viewed it as a fruitful form of love?

This is also only a partial sketch of those reasons. I will offer five possible meanings or purposes of celibacy, all of which are discussed in Christian tradition.

These might not be the most important aspects of celibacy for you. Other meanings abound. For example, people nowadays sometimes talk about celibacy as a countercultural witness to the depth of nonsexual bonds, or a revolt against the commodification of love (including gay love—all those businesses draped in rainbow flags, all those Wells Fargo floats at Pride). I sometimes think that celibacy is one way of preserving the mystery of our bodies: letting them be strange and even baffling, rather than demanding that they be useful. In this way celibacy can be a revolt against the busy, practical world; it can be a reminder that our bodies are icons, not tools.

Patricia Grey, the founder of the National Black Sisters' Conference and formerly a Religious Sister of Mercy, once said that "to be celibate, black, and committed gives promise and danger to life."[4] Celibacy for the kingdom of God can be a witness against all those who believed your body could be their property, your consent irrelevant. It can have all the joy of revolt against injustice, performed in and consecrated to nonviolence.

I won't do anything with those ideas here, but maybe you should.

The five purposes I'll discuss intertwine at times, but I think it makes sense to talk about them separately. This way, I can emphasize different aspects of experiences that in any individual's life and spirituality may be closely linked.

What I hope to do, above all, is to offer an *approach*: a way of evaluating theories and theologies of celibacy in light of what they might offer to you as you try to live celibately. I have two basic structuring ideas. First, several of the purposes of celibacy I present here hold dangers for gay Christians, as well as certain opportunities for us, and I want to note the pitfalls as well as the promises. Second, I've organized these purposes so that they work inward and upward: inward to the heart of Christ and upward to heaven.

Unchosen Blessings

One final preliminary note, about language. I am using "celibacy" here in a colloquial rather than technical meaning. I mean, essentially, people who are unmarried and have no intention of marrying. Celibacy, then, is an arena of love characterized by renunciation of sex and marriage.

The discussion that follows is not dependent on your reasons for finding yourself in this state of life. There's a lot of loose talk nowadays about how celibacy is (or should be) a "gift" or a "calling" you discern *within yourself*. But often God calls us through the unchosen circumstances of our lives. Aging parents, addiction and recovery, the baptism you received before you could even form memories—these circumstances shape our lives. They close off some avenues but open other opportunities to love, often ones we would not have chosen for ourselves. So, too, our sexual orientation may shape the ways we love, in ways we wouldn't have chosen for ourselves.

None of that is an argument for what you should do; I've tried not to make this book too much of an argument for obedience to Catholic teaching. But I do want to suggest that our cultural attachment to ideas of "choice" can make it harder for us to see how God is working in the unchosen circumstances of our lives. When Christians argue that the only good celibacy is "voluntary" celibacy rather than "mandated" celibacy, they gloss over the degree to which all our choices are constrained by the interaction of circumstances and conviction.

I'm not "good at" celibacy and I would not have chosen it for myself. I don't perceive a special call to it. Over time I think I'm learning to love it, but that's because I've accepted it.

The title of this section, "Unchosen Blessings," was inspired by a qualitative study of women living in a homeless shelter. These women chose to bring unintended (often unwanted) pregnancies to term and found blessings in that experience alongside the stigma, poverty, fear, and pain.[5] Many gay Christians have to go through a grueling journey to the self-acceptance which allows them to acknowledge that being gay, while not something they chose, is a source of blessing in their lives. I hope this book can make that journey faster and those blessings brighter. I also hope this book, and specifically this chapter, can make it easier for gay Christians to accept celibacy: to find self-acceptance in celibacy, rather than viewing life without sex as purely a deprivation or even a punishment for being gay. I hope it will help readers to experience the blessings that can come with celibacy whether you've yearned for it or feared it, and even if you're still struggling to come to terms with it.

Christian celibacy is service and sacrifice and ecstasy; it is obedience and freedom. Which of these aspects of celibacy will be most prominent in your own life is determined mostly by circumstance and the frankly bizarre will of God, not by your choice.

So now, five purposes of celibacy, no matter what your reasons are.

1. Celibacy allows us to give ourselves more fully to our community.

> Authentic celibacy—whether lay, ordained, or vowed—is oriented toward social and community life. To be a "spiritual father" or "spiritual mother"—perhaps as a member of the clergy or religious, but also as a godparent, or an adopted relative, or a catechist or teacher, or simply as a mentor and friend—is an esteemed vocation, something essential for a healthy and flourishing Christian community. . . . [C]elibacy is a communal practice.
> —Catholic Archdiocese of Philadelphia,
> *Love Is Our Mission: The Family Fully Alive*[6]

> Bear one another's burdens, and so you
> will fulfill the law of Christ.
>
> —Galatians 6:2

The most community-minded purpose of celibacy is that celibacy frees (or pushes!) us to form and strengthen kinds of relationships that might otherwise go neglected. This is the purpose I see most obviously in my own life, since I am a Martha and not a Mary, I'm sorry to say. Celibate people are godparents, friends (including covenant friends), monks and nuns and priests. The celibate gay people I know include crisis-pregnancy counselors, adoptive and foster parents, "aunties," and caregivers to aging parents. They include members of intentional communities, with relationships to those most in need. They include mentors to LGBT teens, school-teachers, and hospital volunteers. And as I learned at the Revoice conference (see part IV) to my gratitude and delight, celibate gay people include pastors in children's ministry.

So much great Christian fiction (*Kristin Lavransdatter*, *The Brothers Karamazov*, and that grande dame of gay Christian lit, *Brideshead Revisited*) shows secular life taking place in the shadow of the monastery. Monastics are in community not only with one another but with all those for whom they offer prayer. In the same way celibate laypeople can provide havens, for one another and for married people. Our work and our prayer can provide refuge.

Celibate people may have greater freedom or autonomy than married people or parents. Celibacy has sometimes given me flexibility, availability, freedom, and even a kind of disposability that has helped me to serve others. When I lived by myself, I was able to offer my home to people in need of a safe place to spend the night, and I could offer it on a whim. If I met a woman who had nowhere to sleep, I could just offer her my apartment without checking with anybody else.

But—living alone was awful for me! Living alone protected my alcoholism. What this positive vision of celibacy calls freedom and autonomy, many people call isolation. This isolation breeds anxiety about the future (who will care for me when I'm old?) and makes many sins, including sins of lust, much more likely. And so it's important to say that celibacy also gives us freedom to form thick, entangling bonds. Someone who is fostering children, caring for aging parents, or living in a covenant friendship isn't autonomous. Some of these entangling bonds make it easier to open your home to people in need; some of these bonds make it harder.

Even hermits, I have learned, often had friends. You could be hermits together. Hermits *a deux*! Some might call this cheating, but I say, no man is an island—even when the island is Patmos.

My own celibate life is more patchwork and precarious than a life embedded in a monastery or adorned with the promises of a covenant friendship. I love my friends and serve my communities; I do none of it as well as I should, but all of it better than I could without the sacraments. Others' gay, celibate lives are more stable—Tim Otto writes beautifully about his life in an intentional community, for example, and the bloggers at *A Queer Calling* have written about their life in celibate partnership.[7]

I wanted to make sure to talk about this purpose of celibacy in part because it is by far the easiest one to figure out how to *do*: keep a place at your table for Elijah (or for the homeless person whom you may encounter during the day), find a community that serves the neediest and start the process of investigating and maybe joining it, take your friends' kids whenever you can so that their parents can get a break—you may not be able to do all or any of this, but if you can, it may help. I've patched together a celibate life with duct tape, and I love it; I love the many ways I've been allowed to serve. For people who are experiencing celibacy as isolation, opening your life to those in need may meet some of your own deepest needs (or, better, help you know and trust that Jesus is enough for all your needs, instead of just constantly lecturing yourself about how he *should* be enough).

Gay people may be especially drawn toward these forms of love through our longing for same-sex love (e.g., women's community, women's friendship). We may also know others' loneliness well.

But there is also one way in which this purpose of celibacy holds especial dangers for us: this is the only purpose of celibacy that relies on *other people* to respond to you. Offering unconventional love is risky in the best circumstances. There's potential for disappointment, misunderstanding, resentment, entitlement, rejection, despair, and for using other people as medicine for your own hurts. There's potential for messiness, is what I'm saying. And gay people run a greater risk of rejection in many Christian communities. We have often already received many hard lessons in the dangers of relying on other people to respond well to us, and to our desires to love and serve.

2. Celibacy allows us to give ourselves to God without distraction.

> I should like you to be free of anxieties. An unmarried man is anxious about the things of the Lord, how he may please the Lord. But a married man is anxious about the things of the world, how he may please his wife, and he is divided. An unmarried woman or a virgin is anxious about the things of the Lord, so that she may be holy in both body and spirit. A married woman, on the other hand, is anxious about the things of the world, how she may please her husband. I am telling you this for your own benefit, not to impose a restraint upon you, but for the sake of propriety and adherence to the Lord without distraction.
> —1 Corinthians 7:32–35

God will never reject you! God is always there to receive your love; and perhaps the most obvious purpose of celibacy for Christians is that it frees us not solely to love one another but to love God.

Honestly, I'm not sure anybody has improved on Paul's words, above, in stating this purpose of celibacy.

We can see that the radical availability of the celibate for God should not turn us against close personal relationships. But Christians down through the ages have insisted that celibacy makes unfettered, unencumbered belonging to God alone *easier* than marriage does. That's true of celibacy lived in community too.

And yet when people try to say more than, "We can all think of examples where these words of Paul's are true," we often start to sound like love is a competition. Like either "Celibates love God more than you do!" or "No other love could ever be as distracting as marriage and parenting because no other love could be that intense." So I won't say more! Maybe some of you understand this aspect of celibacy better, and I look forward to hearing your own thoughts on it.

The other danger here, of course, is that it can seem as if we love God more *by* loving other people less. The especial danger for celibate gay people is that our loves and our longing to serve are already so often treated as suspect, and we're told to flee them and "rely on God alone"—meaning, to *be alone* in your walk with God.

However, because we are unlikely to have the relationships that are so often idolized by churches or our culture, it may also be easier for us to see that no human relationship can ever equal the astonishing, all-encompassing love of God. I don't want to skip ahead too much, but we can see in Bernard's face in Ribalta's painting how overwhelming God's love truly is—how much bigger, how much more captivating than the most devoted friendship or the most beautiful marriage. Friendship, marriage, the adoration of a mother for her child: it takes nothing from these loves to say that they are all miniatures, preparations, hints, and clues to the colossal love of God.

3. Celibacy is beautiful because celibacy is a witness to our trust in God and in the resurrection of the dead.

> At the resurrection they neither marry
> nor are given in marriage but are like the
> angels in heaven.
> —Matthew 22:30

In 2017 Pixar released a film, *Coco*, in which a boy journeys to the afterlife after stealing a dead man's guitar. No shade to *Coco*—if you loved the marigold-petal bridge and the living *alebrijes,* and you cried at the ending, I am right there with you—but let's talk for a moment about the afterlife in *Coco.*[8]

Coco melds Mexican traditions and folk belief with the film-makers' own inventions. The *ofrendas*, altars commemorating and welcoming the souls of the dead, are real—and beautifully depicted. But the filmmakers transform some traditions into "rules" of the movie's world, and they make subtle changes to other beliefs, adding up to a movie that's weirdly disturbing if you think about it too long.

In *Coco* you continue to live on as long as someone remembers you. As long as someone decorates an altar for you on the Day of the Dead, you remain alive. But this afterlife replicates the inequalities of our life on earth, instead of overturning them as we see in the parable of Lazarus and the rich man (Lk 16:19–31). The *Coco* heaven has not sainthood but celebrity, and not servanthood but slums. The more you're remembered and loved by the living, the wealthier you are. And if there is no one left to place your picture on an altar . . . you dissolve and disappear forever.

In *Coco* family is central. Your family will remember you. Your family *must* remember you. They are the legacy you leave behind you, to protect yourself in the afterlife; they are your immortality.

This is the kind of world into which Jesus came. It is like the world where family tombs lined the Roman roads; it is like the world into which Christian sexual renunciates, the vowed virgins and the early monastics and even married couples who gave up sex, entered like strange, stripped, dancing skeletons, part *memento mori* and part jester. The Christians still loved and remembered their dead, but they rejected the Roman idea that our immortality depends on our family line. All of us can live again! Our immortality exists already, in Jesus Christ.

Peter Brown, in his terrific 1988 study *The Body and Society: Men, Women, and Sexual Renunciation in Early Christianity*, captures the threat that Christian celibacy posed to the Roman social order: "To join the hermits in the forest-clad mountains of the Black Sea, or to vanish among the caves in the tufa-rock gulleys that lay at a temptingly short distance from Cappadocia, was worse than shocking; it caused the cold shadow of death to fall across the future of whole families. For young males, the potential fathers of noble families, to meditate sexual renunciation was to meditate social extinction."[9]

There is a recklessness to Christian celibacy, and this is a major part of its witness. In celibacy we proclaim that our inheritance and our legacy are in God alone. We do not need to leave anything behind us here.

This is a hard saying. I had the joy of attending my nephew's bar mitzvah. My father passed the Torah scrolls to his son-in-law, who passed the scrolls to his son. This is not a scene that would have taken place if I were my parents' only child. Celibate people can leave legacies (St. Aelred's spiritual children may outnumber the sons of Genghis Khan), but in the end we proclaim with our bodies that our hope is in the Lord and that our immortality is in the resurrection and not in the family line.

This is a hard saying—but also a hopeful saying. Christian celibacy proclaims that marriage and children do not define our purpose. Marriage and children do not fulfill God's will *better than* a life without these blessings—because the celibate life offers another, unique blessing. Even the unlucky, the despised, and the obscure are all capable of loving in the way that we will love in heaven.

Like the resurrection of Jesus—whom St. Methodius called *archiparthenos*, the Arch-Virgin[10]—the lives of Christian celibates witness to our hope in the life of the world to come.

For in heaven, in the eternal life of union with God, there is neither marrying nor giving in marriage. Heaven is the height of love, and heaven is without marriage; therefore celibacy must be a possible arena of love. Celibate people, no matter what our reasons for unmarriage, offer a prefiguration of the kind of love we hope to know forever, when our journey here is done.

This life of heaven is a life of communal love—love offered to God, above all, and overflowing to embrace all people. In this way celibacy as witness to the reality of heaven can strengthen the first and second purposes I discussed, celibacy as availability to the community and celibacy as availability to God. We were created male and female; this creation was good, and marriage seems like a pretty obvious way of honoring its goodness. But Jesus promises that there are other ways of honoring the beautiful creation of our bodies. He calls us to imagine a life *beyond* marriage. In the kingdom of heaven—which is, above all, the kingdom of love—we will all love as celibates, in our resurrected bodies. And the kingdom of heaven is at hand.

By sacrificing the form of love and family that our culture tells us to want (whether that's heterosexual marriage only or gay marriage also), we proclaim our trust that Jesus' promise of heaven is true. The sacrifice is absurd, unless Jesus is faithful.

The great difficulty here for gay people is that our experiences in the churches have made trust in God and his promises much harder. When the same church that seems to impose celibacy on us as a burden or even a punishment for being gay then turns around and says, "It's a beautiful sign of your trust in God!" both trust and celibacy become much harder and can even become forms of self-harm. Moreover, offering us an inheritance in heaven may become a way for churches to let themselves off the hook of supporting us in this life.

On the other hand—and this is more of a personal opinion than most of what I'm trying to do in this chapter, but it's my book so you get my opinions—you know what is super nice about celibacy as foreshadowing or witnessing to the love we'll know in heaven? It calls into question the idea that we need to pass through heterosexuality on the way to eternal bliss. Why can't I skip the part where I want to have sex with men, if that's just leading to this love that is *beyond* marriage? Why not long directly for the love of heaven and prepare myself for it through growing in celibacy?

4. Celibacy is beautiful because celibacy is a form of poverty.

> Do not store up for yourselves treasures on earth, where moth and decay destroy, and thieves break in and steal. But store up treasures in heaven, where neither moth nor decay destroys, nor thieves break in and steal. For where your treasure is, there also will your heart be.
>
> —Matthew 6:19–21

In celibacy we renounce a good that our Lord also renounced. We experience a loss, an ache, a privation. This privation should not be destitution—that's something our church *should* help us with. The poverty of a monk should not be desperate, should not be starvation, and the same is true with celibacy. But celibacy is a renunciation of a good and a form of surrender.

In contemporary America, lay celibates also renounce the social status people often gain (especially in our churches) through marriage. We have made marriage and family an idol. We've made the married people winners—we even often consider it irresponsible to marry before you achieve personal and economic stability (those

ever-receding horizons), so marriage is reserved for the lucky spin-
ners of late capitalism's Wheel of Fortune.[11] And the unmarried
people are left as losers, asking loser questions like, *Who will care
for me when I'm old? What if my friends move away? What do I do
with my urgent desire for sex? How can I give my love, and who will
want it?*

I'm not saying married people have it easy; they desperately
need our support, including our economic support. But there are
ways in which being married is *a little* like being rich, in the sense
that many people think of you as having something honorable
and desirable and think of lack of marriage as a failure. This is an
un-Christian attitude (toward literal wealth, too), but it is one reason that our obedient embrace of celibacy can be a way of "taking
the lowest place," which is always the place closest to Christ.

Understanding celibacy as an arena of love—whether our celibacy is lived in covenant friendship / celibate partnership or in
more ordinary friendships, in monastic community or the ordinary
community of the parish, with a "family of choice" or our family of
origin—topples the hierarchy of winners and losers. All of us who
are willing to lose our lives will gain them, in Christ.

Christopher C. Roberts, in *Creation and Covenant: The Significance of Sexual Difference in the Moral Theology of Marriage*, offers
an insightful diagnosis: "Could it be that expectations of erotic
fulfillment, an attitude of sexual entitlement, is a variation upon
wealth, a new possession modern people grip so tightly that we
cannot be wholehearted followers of Christ? . . . As with the church's
teaching on voluntary poverty, or other types of suffering, a language will have to be recovered, to the effect that there is freedom
and joy in a life without those things the world calls necessary."[12]

But note that Roberts also says, earlier, "The failure of the visible church to be sufficiently countercultural, such that a social life
of lay celibacy is conceivable, is a likely reason [so many Christians
reject the traditional sexual ethic]. We cannot imagine existing in
our culture without the haven of an erotic partnership, because

our capacity to belong together in more chaste ways is so limited." And so our proclamation of our sexual ethic, he says, "seems cruel and laughable."[13]

These two quotations from Roberts capture both the dangers this understanding of celibacy can pose to gay Christians and the ways in which our situation may make us sensitive to celibacy's beauties. The obvious danger here for gay people is that too many churches already tell us we're failures and we deserve deprivation.

The obvious gift we can offer is that, although the churches have often forgotten that Christ lives in those who are *not* successful in the eyes of the world, we remember that truth. Gay communities, at their best, preserve a belief that "we're all in this together" and that we must not retreat into respectability while others remain exposed to humiliation and suffering. For gay Christians who don't have the respectable haven of marriage (including, in increasingly large swathes of society, the respectable haven of gay marriage), this solidarity is all the more necessary. Solidarity with those outside the havens of respectability is imitation of Christ.

5. Celibacy is beautiful because it offers a unique intimacy with Christ. It makes the celibate's body a secret garden, a bridal chamber where God alone enters to tryst with his lover, the Christian soul.

> Now one who asks for a kiss is in love. It is not for liberty that she asks, nor for an award, not for an inheritance nor even knowledge, but for a kiss.
> —St. Bernard of Clairvaux,
> *On the Song of Songs* (Sermon 7)

So if you read enough about celibacy, you notice how often people talk about the unique intimacy with God that celibacy offers.

At least up through the Middle Ages this was a commonplace of Christian discourse. And yet nobody can agree on why!

People come up with all kinds of explanations as to why a certain ecstatic, mystical union with God seems especially available to celibates. Some explanations are rarely heard today. Jews and pagans in the ancient world believed that sex provokes "a warm rush of vital spirits through the body," which blocks up the emptiness you need to receive divine inspiration.[14] Among some early Christians there was a belief that virgins' voices sounded better![15] Some speculated that if you're not distracted by sensual pleasures, including but not limited to the pleasures of sex, your body responds more strongly to the pleasures of union with God in prayer.

But what strikes me about this multitude of explanations, some of which are kind of cuckoo, is that they are attempts to understand a phenomenon everyone had noticed: that people who renounced sex had some kind of unusual access to the Lord. We were in some way vessels, receptive and ready to be filled with God's spirit, exposed to God's caresses. Celibates are naked, the ancient Christians say; we let nothing come between us and the kiss of Christ on our bare souls.

Whatever the mechanism, the celibate makes of her body a secret garden, for God's pleasure alone. The celibate makes of his body a bridal chamber, enclosed, hushed, where his soul can embrace her Lover, her Lord. These encounters are most easily described in erotic imagery; arguably they are what all our experiences of the erotic point us toward, as all our longings are lessons about God. And long before St. Bernard, before even the fall of Rome, Christians noticed that those who had renounced sex and marriage were in some way made more receptive to this burning and quenching in the soul, of which sex and marriage are images.

Note that this giving of one's body to God is about your *choice*, and it can take place at any time in your life. The secret garden or bridal chamber in which you tryst with your Lord is created by your willing gift of yourself in celibacy, so you can create it with your body no matter what has happened to your body before this. A survivor of sexual abuse can create this privacy and give her body in celibacy to God. Someone who has been unchaste in the past may give his body wholeheartedly to God at any point. (A famous example many of you may know is St. Aelred, author of the beautiful dialogues called *Spiritual Friendship* that influenced my discussion of David and Jonathan in chapter 2.[16]) Celibacy is not about virginity-fetishism; it honors and is dependent on your will and your conscience.

This ecstasy is not something I have experienced. The consolations I have received in prayer are normal consolations, an experience of sweetness or a sudden aliveness to the created world. These same hints of love are relatively common among the married and the single (i.e., the not-yet-married) as well as among the celibate.

Moreover, God scatters these *experiences* of bliss unpredictably. He may let you feel the embrace to which you've bared yourself once right away, and then never again for all the long years of your obedience. Or he may not grant you that at all, until you rise to your reward in heaven. It can seem painfully unfair. Service, however, is something you can do right now—you can find a way to serve, through your prayers or your acts. So why not emphasize service, instead of a shattering ecstasy you may never actually perceive?

I emphasize this ecstasy, and structured this chapter around it, because mystical union with Christ is what all the other purposes of celibacy lead up to. This is what they point to. The central purpose of celibacy is its most mysterious: to prepare us for the kiss of Christ.

A Friend Who Cherishes

In the middle of the thirteenth century, a four-year-old girl named Gertrude entered the monastery school at Helfta, in present-day Germany. She spent the rest of her life in the monastery, surrounded by holy women like St. Mechtild, "the Nightingale of Helfta," a visionary and spiritual guide. These women guided Gertrude's education and formed the little girl into the woman we know as St. Gertrude the Great. Like Mechtild (and like Bernard before them), she developed the spirituality of the Christian soul as bride of Christ. Like Bernard she cherished and developed the devotion to the Sacred Heart of Jesus, which, as John the Beloved Disciple told her in a vision, he had felt pulsing as he lay against his Savior's breast at the Last Supper.

Gertrude wrote a prayer that hymns equally obedience to Christ and bliss in his embrace. Gertrude's monastic discipline allowed her to experience what most of us have to hold as truths of the faith, assented to but rarely experienced so ardently: that Christ is both infinite power and infinite gentleness.

> You are the overflowing abyss of divinity,
> Oh king of all kings most worthy,
> Supreme emperor,
> Illustrious prince,
> Ruler of infinite sweetness,
> Faithful protector.
> You are the vivifying gem of humanity's nobility.
> Craftsman of great skill,
> Teacher of infinite patience,
> Counselor of great wisdom,
> Most kind guardian,
> Most faithful friend.
> You are the delicate taste of intimate sweetness.
> Oh most delicate caresser,
> Gentlest passion,
> Most ardent lover,
> Sweetest spouse,
> Most pure pursuer.
> You are the burgeoning blossom of natural beauty.
> Oh most lovable brother,
> Most beautiful youth,

Happiest companion,
Most munificent host,
Most courteous administrator.[17]

Gertrude's Lord is a Christ whose wise counsel is a caress. He orders our hearts *because* he cherishes us. He is not a cover-up artist or a con man. He is an authority who is, if I can put the point most bluntly, not an abuser.

What happens when you realize that the God you were taught to know in childhood is not Gertrude's trustworthy Friend? How can you begin to experience God's tenderness when your church taught you to serve a god of suspicion and self-loathing? Where does scripture speak to the people who love Jesus, even though they barely survived a Christian childhood?

That's the subject of the next two chapters.

Part III

THE
CHURCH
SUFFERING

four

WEAPONIZED CHRISTIANITY

In her 1985 study *The Body in Pain: The Making and Unmaking of the World*, philosopher Elaine Scarry described the way torturers change their victims' understanding of the world:

> The contents of the [torture] room, its furnishings, are converted into weapons: the most common instance of this is the bathtub that figures prominently in the reports from numerous countries, but it is only one among many. Men and women being tortured . . . describe being handcuffed in a constricted position for hours, days, and in some cases months to a chair, to a cot, to a filing cabinet, to a bed; they describe being beaten with "family-sized soft drink bottles" or having a hand crushed with a chair, of having their heads "repeatedly banged on the edges of a refrigerator door." . . . The room . . . is converted into a weapon . . . [M]ade to demonstrate that everything is a weapon, the objects themselves, and with them the fact of civilization, are annihilated: there is no wall, no window, no door, no bathtub, no refrigerator, no chair, no bed.[1]

The tortured person's every action becomes a weapon in the hands of the torturer—from mundane acts such as standing or sitting, to reverent acts such as kneeling or prostrating oneself. These acts, which should honor God, are instead intended to replace God's love with the torturer's contempt. Compare St. Francis's Canticle of the Creatures—"All praise be yours, my Lord, through Sister Water, so useful, lowly, precious and pure"—with this testimony from a survivor of waterboarding: "Nasim, a survivor of waterboarding from Ethiopia, who does not want her last name in the press, says that she is 'brought back to the torture chambers every time I hear the sound of splashing water. In the shower, when water hits my face, I must remind myself that I am not strapped to a board and that my lungs will not fill up with water until I lose consciousness.'"[2] God created the world in his love and sustains it by love. The torturer tries to annihilate this truth and make every aspect of the world speak a lie: the lie that no one loves you and no one hears your screams.

And what many gay Christians at some point realize is that the people who taught them the faith did something similar to the Gospel. They took the words of life, of hope, of peace and hurled them like weapons. Sometimes the weaponization of the Prince of Peace was unintentional. Sometimes it was openly malicious. Parents who beat their kids because they believed coming out was a form of immoral defiance; schoolmates who laughed about how "fags" went to hell; the use of Christian morality to make gay people feel worthless, dirty, shameful, cast out; the slow poison of constant suspicion and insistent interrogations about whether you're masculine enough, feminine enough, too close to your friends, safe around children—all of that is its own anti-catechism. It teaches people the Gospel turned inside out.

This chapter is about coming to know God's tender love for you, when you have been taught this anti-catechism.

The process of learning that God loves and cherishes you is an educational process, and it proceeds more or less the way your original religious education proceeded: with pain—although the pain, I think you'll find, is different in character. It's the pain of cleansing a wound, not creating it.

Here's an oversimplified model. Christianity teaches certain truths: Jesus is the Word made flesh, Jesus died for our sins and rose from the dead, and so on. These truths get lived out among believers in a wide range of practices. Some of those practices are speech acts—the things you say to others, the things you think to yourself, the words you pray. But the practices by which you live out the truths of the faith go far beyond words. Beginning your day with the Bible, making sure to have something to give when someone asks for change, feasting and fasting with the Church, restraining your tongue from gossip, and speaking out when others are mistreated are all everyday practices that flow from the doctrines of the faith. These everyday practices build up habits and shape our imaginations. What we believe about God affects what we do, and what we do affects how we see the world and ourselves.

So far so good. The problem is that most gay Christians grew up learning half-truths about God, at best, or even damaging falsehoods. So gay people who grew up Christian often learned damaging practices (habitual ways of speaking to and behaving toward themselves and God, as well as toward other people) and *didn't* learn the practices that might have helped them to experience God's love for them.

I mean, being real: Can you name *one* daily practice that helps you to trust that God loves you in and through your experience of sexuality?

Gay people too often train ourselves to despise our longing to give and receive love; we hide in the closet and fear other gay people. These practices and habits create imaginations warped by—almost defined by—shame, self-loathing, and fear.

The very first step in reshaping our imaginations, so that they are places illuminated by God's love, is to identify the false beliefs about God that we absorbed unwittingly from our previous religious education.

A few years ago I edited an anthology called *Christ's Body, Christ's Wounds: Staying Catholic When You've Been Hurt in the Church*. One of the contributors, Elena (a pseudonym), told the story of how she confronted the voice in her head, which was not the voice of God:

> I remember one day in the chapel writing down all the things that "Angry Jesus" said to me. Upon rereading

what I had written, I realized that my view of Jesus was more like an abusive boyfriend than a savior or a friend.

I had written,

Your sin is your own fault and I'll only forgive you if you don't do it again. No matter how good your intentions were, you should have known better. I'm just. I owe you nothing. You deserve hell. I was testing you, you failed. You can do all things through Me. That means if you ever do something wrong, it's because you failed. . . . You have to believe everything the church teaches immediately, no hesitation, no questioning. Well, you can question, but there's not a whole lot of point because you know what answer you have to get if you don't want Me to abandon you. I'll never abandon you—as long as you do what I want. Be perfect, like Me. Ohhhh, snap! You can't! Well, maybe if you're really, really, really good and nice to me I'll let you in to heaven. But really, we both know what you really are—say it with Me now—not. good. enough.

Oh, you thought that peace and acceptance you felt earlier was Me? Nah. That was your own delusion again. The truth hurts, baby. And the truth is, I've never loved you. . . .

Sometimes you suspect that I'm not really Jesus at all, that there is a being out there who placed these desperate yearnings in you and Himself yearns to satisfy them with Himself. Who doesn't care how broken or wounded you are, who doesn't need you to do anything except come to Him and who will never cast you out no matter how much you mess up.

But you're too scared to take a chance and that's the way I like it. I own you and there's nothing you can do about it.

I stopped and reread what I had written. Then I wrote, in big block letters,

THIS IS NOT THE VOICE OF GOD.

THIS IS THE VOICE OF THE ACCUSER.

I HAVE LISTENED FAR TOO LONG.

I AM DONE.

I LISTEN ONLY TO THE VOICE OF GOD, THE ONE TRUE GOD.

If He is all-powerful and all-loving, He can and will make me hear His voice. And if not, then I don't want Him anyway. So who is God, really? Start with Ed [my husband]. God cannot be less loving, less forgiving, less generous, less accepting, less faithful than Ed.

That was the beginning of escaping the prison of fear that was built by spiritual abuse.[3]

One of the most desperately necessary tasks for any gay Christian—especially, though not only, one who was raised in a Christian family—is learning to tell the difference between the voice of God and the voice of societal or familial rejection. And this is not just a task set before people whose parents hit them, or who were subjected to homophobic rants from the pulpit. All of us came to our faith in a Christian culture that seemed to make no space for us—in which God seemed to have no future for us.

All of us have this in common: there were times when we treated Jesus as an unloving abuser, because this is who we were taught he was. (We were often taught this unintentionally, by people who only wanted us to know Christ's love and to whom we are still deeply grateful for all they did to show us God's mercy.) We tried to love that idea of Jesus, the way people often try to love those who harm them; we tried to submit ourselves to him, and we told ourselves to be grateful that he was a part of our lives. And all the time, Jesus was trying to tell us, *That is not who I am, because I am Love. I am for you and not against you.*

Naming the falsehoods we were taught is the first step in believing the title of Elena's essay: "Jesus Is Not an Abusive Boyfriend." Once we have identified the false doctrines that "Jesus the abusive boyfriend" shouts at us, we can then identify the ways we've learned to talk to and act toward ourselves, other people, and God, which were shaped by these doctrines. (This is an ongoing task. You'll never be done with the work of discovering that God is better and sweeter to you than you knew.) We can then identify doctrines and practices that might replace these falsehoods and forms of self-harm.

Four Truths

Here are truths of our faith, grounded in scripture. They might be hard to hear. I often find them hard to hear, for reasons that aren't about being gay but are about all the other excuses we find to dislike ourselves. But they are true. For each of these doctrines, it might be worth considering what kind of practice or habit might help you allow them to shape your imagination. I'll suggest some options, but you will likely come up with even more that speak to your own needs and spirituality.

God created you out of love and sustains you solely by his love.

It's divine love that moves your heart to beat and your lungs to breathe. You are here, in this life, because he wants you here. Here's Wisdom 11:24–26:

> For you love all things that are
>   and loathe nothing that you have made;
>   for you would not fashion what you hate.
> How could a thing remain, unless you willed it;
>   or be preserved, had it not been called forth by
>   you?
> But you spare all things, because they are yours,
> O Ruler and Lover of souls,
>   for your imperishable spirit is in all things!

Fr. James Martin, S.J., has a book, *Building a Bridge: How the Catholic Church and the LGBT Community Can Enter into a*

Relationship of Respect, Compassion, and Sensitivity, which includes Bible passages for LGBT people and our friends and families to pray through. You might pick up his book, since he gives a better introduction on how to meditate on scripture than I could! But one passage he cites is worth special attention. Fr. Martin notes, "Of all the passages in the Bible, this one, in my experience, has proven to be the most helpful for LGBT people and their family and friends." It's Psalm 139:1–18, which tells us that God knows us completely, in all our ways, in every aspect of our lives, and he is with us wherever we go; there's nowhere he doesn't hold us, nowhere that his light can't shine. In perhaps the central, most memorable verses, we hear,

> For it was you who formed my inward parts;
>> you knit me together in my mother's womb.
> I praise you, for I am fearfully and wonderfully made.[4]

Among the questions Fr. Martin suggests for our reflection are, "Think about what it means for you to be 'wonderfully made.' Can you praise God, as the psalmist does? What would your praise look like?" He continues, "The psalmist admits that God's ways are beyond the human capacity to understand, and yet the psalmist is 'still with' God. What do you think gives the psalmist that kind of faith?"[5]

I might add that it's worth reflecting on the guarantee we have that these words of scripture are *true.* Then, how do we respond to the truths that we are fearfully and wonderfully made, that God knows us more intimately than we know ourselves and loves us more intensely? How would we *like* to respond to these truths? How do these truths fit into our relationship to scripture?

Beginning the day with this passage, taping it to your bathroom mirror, shoving it in your wallet, or taking a moment each day to reflect on these questions may help you live to the rhythms of God's love.

Rejection by other people doesn't mean that God has rejected you.

Scripture promises us the opposite: when others reject us, including our church or our family, God holds us especially close.

You may have been made to feel outcast and unfit for the kingdom because you're gay. You may have been rejected by church and by family—the places where we should be most sheltered and loved. In these circumstances, scripture offers a word of mercy and acceptance. God knows how his people can treat those they despise, and he has made sure that scripture includes words of comfort for those who are cast out.

In Isaiah chapter 49, God speaks to captive Israel, oppressed in exile in Babylon:

> Can a mother forget her infant,
>> be without tenderness for the child of her womb?
> Even should she forget,
>> I will never forget you.

With these words the Bible acknowledges that some people *are* rejected by their own families, but reminds them that God will not reject or forget them: "See, upon the palms of my hands I have engraved you" (Is 49:16a).

Again and again, scripture insists that those who are rejected or scorned by respectable society are especially close to God. In Matthew 21:42 Jesus quotes Psalm 118:

> Jesus said to them, "Did you never read in the scriptures:
>> 'The stone that the builders rejected
>>> has become the cornerstone;
>> by the Lord has this been done,
>>> and it is wonderful in our eyes'?"

Here the rejected stone is Christ himself, regarded with suspicion by the very people who believe themselves closest to the Lord.

Scripture is full of examples of people who were wrongly accused and cast out by respectable people who believed they were doing God's will. Susannah was falsely accused by the respectable men of her community; they accused her of unchastity in order to protect their own reputations and prevent their own evils from being exposed (Dn 13). Job among his false comforters and the "suffering servant" of Isaiah were closer to God than the respectable, right-living, successful people who refused to care for them. And Christ was persecuted by the leaders of God's own people and betrayed by his disciple Judas.

When your own church has acted more like Judas to you than like Jesus, Jesus promises that he understands your pain and cherishes you. When your church was a mixture of both betrayer and savior—sometimes the most confusing situation of all—Jesus promises that he will walk with you through your confusion. He is not the abusive boyfriend but the Good Shepherd. He will defend you and guide you.

God is not absent in any of your longings for love. He is working in your yearning for same-sex love.

That doesn't mean he's gonna (necessarily) find you a covenant friend or celibate partner, let alone the kind of life your mom or your catechism teacher would understand. We aren't promised intelligible lives. We aren't promised anything we ourselves would recognize as success—quite the opposite. But we are promised that all our loves point upward, beyond themselves, toward God: the source and summit of all love.

Here are a few practices I've developed that help me experience my same-sex desires in holy and fruitful ways. When I notice my head turning to look at a lady on the street—or in any other circumstance where I'm momentarily charmed or deeply awed by the beauty of a woman—I take a moment to thank God for her and for her beauty. He created it. He gave me the gift of seeing it. The proper response to this beauty isn't lust—but neither is it right to pretend you just don't notice the loveliness God has scattered so prodigiously through our world. You can be grateful that you notice, instead of ashamed.

I started this practice as a way to learn chastity. It definitely helped with that, but (uh, as you'll see in a few chapters) I still "struggle with chastity." Nonetheless, this practice made me far more at peace with God. An experience that might have provoked anxiety and self-doubt now provokes gratitude and trust that there's a good way to live out all the longings he has given me. An experience that might have heightened a painful ambivalence now reminds me of the possibility of harmony between my heart and my Lord—a harmony that will always have some discord in this life, but in which I can participate more deeply day by day.

I've also sought out ways to give more in my relationships with women, both friendships and relationships of service. I wrote in *Gay and Catholic* about the ways my longing for women's community led me to volunteer at a crisis pregnancy center. That was one, admittedly kinda weird, answer to the question, "How can I live out, instead of suppressing, my desire to love and serve women?"

Simply asking yourself that question (or its gay dude equivalent) may open up some new pathways for you. Asking questions like, "Where is God working in my experience of being gay? What is beautiful in my longings, and how can I respond to the beauty which God has allowed me to perceive in others?" may suggest practices, as well as things to recall to yourself when you feel hopeless or consumed by shame.

A friend of mine sent me an email a little while back saying, "I was praying my Examen this morning and a point came up that I wanted to ask you about. St. Ignatius basically says that if you're truly grateful for a gift, you won't misuse it. That got me thinking that maybe I'm not so grateful for my sexual desires. Like I'm not (as) upset about my orientation [as I used to be], but I do have a good bit of confusion about why I have desires if I can't use them. What do you think?"

I wrote back, "I like your interpretation of St. I a lot. There are probably many different ways to be grateful for one's sexual desires; we can be grateful for what connects us to others, for what we're called to sacrifice, for the love and mercy we discover when we turn to God in confusion (even if we don't get answers, we do get mercy . . .); and of course one can be grateful for how pretty ladies are, LOL. . . . I'd be interested in what other possibilities come to mind for you."

So that is another question you can ask yourself: *What would it look like to be grateful to be gay? What in these experiences can I be grateful for even now, and what are some areas where being grateful is challenging but imaginable?*

God isn't out to get you.

He isn't trying to trip you up or trick you. He knows how hard this stuff is—how complex it is to understand, how difficult it is to accept in a world where so much Christian "witness" is really counterwitness, and how painful and uncertain it often feels to live.

God sees your rationalizations and ambivalence, yes, but he also sees and cherishes your honesty, your perseverance, and your willingness to turn again to him with your questions and fears. He didn't let you experience sexuality in this way as a kind of trap, to force you into sin or push you away from him—in fact, he has made ways, however hard they are to see, by which your experience of being gay can bring you closer to him. He trusts that you can love him and that you want to (even if you also want other things).

God knows you better and more unsparingly than you know yourself. And, knowing you, he views you not with suspicion but with tenderness.

Can you take a moment to look at yourself with that tenderness? How would you seem to yourself if you removed all the suspicion, anger, and shame? How would you look to someone who cherishes you?

These four truths (that God created you out of love, is on your side when others abandon you, is working in all your longings, and isn't out to get you) are only starting points. All four truths focus on God's nature and actions. There's no need for and little point in focusing on your own personal qualities. Sometimes in various forms of self-help or therapy we're asked to repeat "affirming" phrases—*I'm good, I'm strong,* or what have you. There are probably ways to understand these phrases that are in line with Christian doctrine: "I'm strong," for example, can sometimes call our attention to how much we've already overcome and survived, and it can give us gratitude and courage to face the future.

But focusing on your own qualities always risks two opposite dangers. If you believe these positive affirmations, you run the risk of thinking the good things in your life (friendships, sobriety, perseverance—anything you can point to, including survival) are things you accomplished on your own, because of your good qualities. This distracts you from God's love, from his work in your life, and from your total reliance on his strength. It can also sometimes feed the normal human tendency to judge others and come up with self-righteous explanations for why other people's lives aren't like ours.

On the other hand, if you *don't* believe these affirmations, now you're trying to convince yourself of something you believe to be false. This is not good preparation for the unflinching honesty that Christian life requires (maybe especially gay Christian life, up against the temptations of the closet). Lots of people just check out at this point and refuse to try—I avoided "cognitive behavioral therapy" for a long time, for example, because I thought it was mostly a matter of telling the mirror that I'm good enough, I'm smart enough, and gosh darn it, people *like* me.[6] This just left me muttering, "I am not good enough! This is obvious! This is *why Jesus died.* Come on!"

Not everybody reacts like this. Other people—arguably, more humble and less combative people—are willing to live by the generally correct theory that repeating self-affirmations helps you to love and serve others better than constantly repeating to yourself that you're worthless and unable to help anybody. If you are able to trust the people who tell you that they see love and strength in you, you may be able to use this kind of self-affirmation as a way to build your trust and hope, which will likely help you trust and hope in God.

I hope that we can get the best of both worlds by repeating the truth about the work God is doing in our fabulously gay lives. People who resist "positive self-talk" don't have to do it. You can simply speak positively about God, who is all-good—but speak positively about him in a way you never expected. All repeated prayers, including our constant refuge in praying the words of scripture, are a form of "cognitive behavioral therapy" insofar as they teach and train our minds, shaping how we see ourselves and others. Finding prayers that help you see God's tenderness toward you as a gay person, and repeating these prayers every day, will reshape your relationship with him.

True Lies

"You mean everybody is *crazy?*"
"In a way of speaking, Bliss. Because the
only logic and sanity is the logic and sanity of God, and down here it's been turned
wrong-side out and upside down. You have
to watch yourself, Bliss, in a situation like
this. Otherwise you won't know what's
sense and what's foolishness. Or what's to
be laughed at and what's to be cried over.
Or if you're yourself or what somebody
says you are."
—Ralph Ellison, *Juneteenth*[7]

Christian homophobia means that gay people hear, over and over
again, many true things that are said in ways or in contexts that
make them lies. As we acknowledge the mistreatment we've experienced at the hands of Christians, and try to heal from it, we face
a baffling problem: How do we untangle the true things we were
taught from the cruelty? When the people who taught us what love
is didn't love us well, by what standard can we judge?

This is also a problem for those who love us, and want to love
us well. It's easy to say a well-meaning thing, which is even true, but
which nonetheless calls forth reflexive anger and pain in gay people
because we've heard the same truths (or clichés) used against us.
I'll list a few common weaponized truths here, but it's impossible
to anticipate all the ways Christianity can be turned into a tool of
abuse. Honestly, you will probably have to be patient a lot of the
time and give your loved ones the benefit of the doubt when they
trot out some bumper-sticker psalm.

"Love the sinner, hate the sin." Or the rebranded version, "God loves you too much to leave you as you are."

This stuff is true! God's love transforms us. It turned Saul the persecutor into Paul the martyr. And paradoxically, in transforming us God's love makes us more truly ourselves—as Dunstan Thompson's later poetry discerned. Our sins aren't who we are, so loving us can't mean loving our sins.

But the thing is, mostly these two clichés are uttered when you've just said you're gay, and a well-meaning Christian tells you God loves you too much to leave you as you are (i.e., a big flamer). Sometimes the straight Christian draws an analogy to their own life. "Before I got saved, I ate babies for breakfast, with a side of LSD! I had four wives and one of them was a donkey! But God changed my heart, and I know he will change yours too."

The thing is that being gay is not very much like eating a baby. It needn't involve sin at all; when it does, the sin may be interwoven with the kind of selfless love that builds homes, welcomes strangers, cares for children, and teaches us about God's love for us. Many of us now know people in gay marriages, people who are in fact committing sexual sin and who believe heresy, yet whose relationships are suffused with self-giving, nurturing love.

When Christians draw analogies between being gay and (to use two bad analogies I've used myself in former times) struggling with anger, or alcoholism, we sound like *all* we can see in homosexuality or same-sex marriage is sin. That makes it much harder to guess how same-sex love might be lived out well.

If you desperately need an analogy, which is like saying what this minefield really needs is a good grenade, may I suggest religious differences? I don't believe Lutheranism is the best response to Christ—you're shocked, I know—but it's obvious that Lutherans can love God and one another, and lots of them do it better than lots of Catholics. The differences between Lutheranism and Catholicism are fearsomely important, but we also have a lot in common and can work together in the areas where our response to the Gospel is similar. Gay marriage and gay sex are the wrong responses to our longings, but those longings are often as complex and as intent on love as our response to the Gospel.

"Don't set limits on God's power!"

This is another one that always means God might turn you straight. You might awake one morning from uneasy dreams to find yourself transformed in your bed into a gigantic heterosexual! (Poor Kafka.)

When churches don't know how to shepherd gay people, they resort to this fantasy that we might just dissolve into the straight majority. Then they could marry us off. We could become like them, and then they won't have to change.

I suspect that God's love will work painful changes in *all* of our lives, not just the gay ones. God loves our churches too much to leave them as they are!

"You are not defined by your sexuality. You are a beloved child of God!"

I mean, I'm not defined by my nationality, either, but nobody thinks it's weird if I say I'm an American, even though God knows *that's* a cause of a lot of sin in the world today.

An important truth lurking in this statement is that *other Christians* so often have treated gay people as if we are defined solely by our sexuality—by sexual sin. The suspicion we face in our churches and the constant assumptions that everything we do is sexual, or that all our problems are the result of being gay, do immense damage in part because they define us by our sexuality and lead us to shape our relationship with God around fear of our sexuality. We are beloved children of God, and so our relationship with him will work through and in every aspect of our lives, including but not limited to our sexuality.

"Homosexuality is just a social construct."

This, I think, is more common among conservative Catholics. The Protestants get more into how you can't limit God's power; Catholics always think we can translate the Christian sexual ethic into *secularese*. Anyway, this statement is mostly true but not *quite* as true as its proponents (I'm one, really) think. And although it's often deployed in order to discredit gay liberation movements, exploring the degree to which this statement is true will actually illuminate the goods that gay movements cherish. Homosexuality is a social construct, and it got constructed for reasons that mean that gay communities have gifts and insights to offer the churches.

Societies have organized our desires and longings in different ways. If you by some impossibility had been born in twelfth-century France, for example, you may not have ever reached the point of considering doing acts prohibited in the Letter to the Romans. You might turn the kaleidoscope of your heart and read the patterns there (which today you read as lesbianism) as a desire to be a nun, or a need to spend as much time as possible with your best friend . . . or a belief that you were born in the wrong body and should have been a man. These are all interpretations of complex feelings, attempts to articulate some desires that your culture would honor and some that it would try to make unspeakable. "Being gay" is a contemporary umbrella term, which covers a hugely diverse set of experiences, from the heterosexually married woman who seeks out "discreet" ladies on a hookup app to the celibate who pours out his life in service and deep friendship.

The seeds of the modern concept of "homosexuality" can be found even in the ancient world. The idea that two men or two women might have a sexual relationship of equals, and consider themselves soulmates, is in Plato's *Symposium*.[8] There are disparaging references in late Roman texts to same-sex weddings, which suggests that at least some ancient people probably thought of their same-sex relationships as similar to marriage.[9] Even in cultures that typically cared much more about, for example, who penetrated and who was penetrated, it was possible to imagine homosexual relationships that look roughly familiar to us. But these are hints and possibilities, in cultures whose norms still connected sex, love, and personal identity in ways truly foreign to us. How did hints and possibilities become a social and political movement?

I find it suggestive that the contemporary gay movement was born in the late nineteenth century—*after* devoted same-sex friendship had lost its public honor, guidance, and protection. If devoted, intimate same-sex friendship is no longer an honorable and recognizable form of life-shaping love, the people who still want to shape their lives around love of someone of the same sex may need fairly urgent motivations to step outside the bourgeois nuclear-family model. Sexual desire provides one such urgent motivation. Martin Duberman's "novel/history" *Jews Queers Germans*, which explores the cultural world of Germany's pre–World War II gay rights movement, makes it seem as if by the early twentieth century sodomy was just about the only way for a man to make a friend![10]

To radically oversimplify: In late nineteenth and early twentieth-century Europe and America, the decline of same-sex friendship meant that any devoted or "romantic" same-sex friendship became suspect—with the exception of wartime, when men were still allowed to love one another. This *suspicion* of same-sex love, enforced by the guardians of normalcy, shaped the modern gay rights movement as the last haven of same-sex devotion.

To the extent that "homosexuality" is a modern social construct, deconstructing it would require honoring same-sex love and affection, rather than holding it in suspicion. This would require real changes in the culture and practices of most churches. What would a church look like in which "homosexuality" is genuinely deconstructed, and the important terms have reemerged as chaste love (good) and sexual sin (bad)? That would be a church where sharing your home and life with a same-sex partner is unremarkable, where covenants or promises of friendship unite people as

Ruth and Naomi were united, where men don't have to act like one another's bodies are made of lava, where butch women aren't objects of suspicion but just gals who don't spend a lot of time on their hair. In this church all holy expressions of same-sex love would be honored and supported. Where same-sex love was expressed in sinful ways, the lovers would be guided not to stop loving but to love each other better. I have never attended such a church.

One way to tell when the social-construct argument is being abused is to ask what we're supposed to do about it. Nine times out of ten, your straight conservative interlocutor thinks you should stop calling yourself gay, considering yourself part of a gay community, and being gay in ways that straight Christians might have to notice and think about. In exchange, they might agree to stop calling themselves "heterosexual"—though of course no one could expect them to stop wearing their wedding ring, or talking about their fiancée, or using their spouse's employer-provided health insurance. As long as you agree to make it harder to talk about your life, they'll agree to make it harder to talk about their privilege.

Here's a decent rule of thumb: When a truth is being spoken in order to pressure only a marginalized group to change, with no change expected of the majority, the truth becomes a falsehood.

The Most Important Thing

I've seen people take many different paths after they come to the realization that some aspects of the Christianity they grew up in deeply harmed them—especially aspects relating to their sexuality and sexual ethic. Some people found ways to re-understand their faith and their celibacy, and they ended up living both faith and celibacy in ways they never expected. They radically reassessed and reshaped their faith, but didn't change their sexual ethic substantially. Some people entered new churches with different sexual ethics and are now in gay marriages or pursuing that path. Some people held a progressive sexual ethic for a while, or flirted with it, but then returned to a traditional one. Some people were just great big messes who slept around and felt awful about it. Some people were literally every single one of these people at different times in their journey.

Jesus knows how hard it is for you to see him through the screen of lies and silences Christians have built to hide his face. The most important thing about all these people—and all these possible outcomes for you if you have to go through the hard journey out of an abusive Christianity—is that Jesus' mercy never fails. It is poured out on all these people. It is the most important fact about their lives and their deeds.

The Example of Mary

Scripture offers a portrayal of what it looks like to humble yourself in total surrender to God's will, while rejecting the structures that oppress you. Scripture even hints at the community and acceptance that can shelter and nurture our obedience to God.

Perhaps the most beautiful song of praise to God in scripture is Mary's Magnificat:

> And Mary said:
>   "My soul proclaims the greatness of the Lord;
>   my spirit rejoices in God my savior.
>   For he has looked upon his handmaid's lowliness;
>   behold, from now on will all ages call me blessed.
>   The Mighty One has done great things for me,
>   and holy is his name.
>   His mercy is from age to age
>   to those who fear him.
>   He has shown might with his arm,
>   dispersed the arrogant of mind and heart.
>   He has thrown down the rulers from their thrones
>   but lifted up the lowly.

> The hungry he has filled with good things;
>   the rich he has sent away empty.
> He has helped Israel his servant,
>   remembering his mercy,
> according to his promise to our fathers,
>   to Abraham and to his descendants forever." (Lk
>   1:46–55)

Mary, at this point in her life, is young and poor and pregnant —and she's in that situation because she accepted a call from God that nobody else had received and that others around her couldn't fully understand. The angel has to tell her, "Do not be afraid" (Lk 1:30)—angels in the Bible always have to tell us this, because whatever they say is frightening at first. Mary willingly (her consent is emphasized in Luke's gospel) gives her body and her future to the Lord, saying, "Behold, I am the handmaid of the Lord. May it be done to me according to your word" (Lk 1:38).

Her Magnificat is, therefore, an outpouring of praise from one who has given everything, believed everything, and done all that she has been asked to do, even when it went against her expectations and the expectations of her society. She might have imagined that bearing the Messiah would bring her honor or riches; instead she's still poor, and decent-living religious people might even be gossiping about how Joseph's bride wound up pregnant before their nuptials. In this way Mary can understand the situation of gay Christians asked to sacrifice not solely sex (although that isn't a trivial sacrifice for most of us) but marriage and the economic security and social honor it often provides. Mary can understand what it's like to make these sacrifices without the understanding or support of most of our fellow Christians.

Mary is a model of acceptance of God's will. She is not, however, a model of knuckling under or accepting *injustice*. And it's worth noticing that she proclaims God's glory when she has finally found someone, other than her patient spouse, who can understand and accept her situation: her relative Elizabeth, who is also experiencing a miraculous pregnancy. Elizabeth greets her with the words we know from the Hail Mary: "Elizabeth, filled with the holy Spirit, cried out in a loud voice and said, 'Most blessed are you among women, and blessed is the fruit of your womb. And how does this happen to me, that the mother of my Lord should come to me? For at the moment the sound of your greeting reached my ears, the infant in my womb leaped for joy'" (Lk 1:41–44).

Elizabeth not only welcomes Mary without judgment, but recognizes the work God is doing in Mary's life—the work most others can't see. She is guided by the Holy Spirit to honor Mary, and so Mary finds a haven with her.

I'm sure Mary could have—and did—praise God from the very beginning of her pregnancy. But it's perhaps important that Luke gives us the Magnificat at a time when Mary is welcomed and understood. She can be a model for the many gay people who are only able to praise God and to see him as truly on our side once we are among people who welcome us rather than judge and reject us. It's in the shelter of solidarity, provided by someone who shares some of Mary's strange experiences, that Mary pours out her praise.

And this praise is not for a God who reshaped her to better fit her society. Quite the opposite. Mary doesn't praise God for making her acceptable to others. She praises him for overturning all the categories by which humans judge one another. God will lift up those who have suffered—and, this scary part we always hasten past—he will cast down those in power.

All of us have power over somebody and all of us have been, at one time or another, "the mighty" who must be cast down from our thrones, "the proud" whose conceit and self-righteousness must be broken. But these images have special resonance for gay people who have been shamed and rejected by their religious communities. People who have been told to repent of something they never chose can hear, in the Magnificat, that it is those who mistaught and mistreated them who most urgently need repentance. People who were taunted in school hallways can hear God call them beloved.

And if they were the ones who did the taunting—since not every gay person has the blessing and protection of being an obvious homo—they can learn from the Magnificat the other way we're called to say yes to God: by admitting wrong, humbling ourselves, and being grateful that the Lord has cast us down from thrones of denial or deceit.

In this way scripture offers hope both to those who are rejected and to those who know that they've rejected others. Our churches are havens for collaborators, communities full of people who have mistreated one another. But if the lion wants to lie down with the lamb, sometimes the lamb's gotta work through some serious issues first. Reconciliation often comes as part of a long wrestling with anger and grief—whether we're talking about reconciliation with God, with the Church as the mystical Body of Christ, with the specific churches we attend or used to attend on Sunday, or with ourselves. That's the subject of the next chapter.

five

IF I'M CELIBATE, CAN I STILL FLIRT WITH ANGER?

Discovering God's tenderness toward you as a gay Christian is joyful and beautiful—but it can also be deeply painful. The path to hope leads through a lot of anger and uncertainty. It's true that you'll never be done discovering how good God has been to you. It may also take a *very* long time before you're done discovering all the falsehoods you were taught about the Lord, all the well-meaning ways you were harmed. Psychologist Alan Downs called his book on "overcoming the pain of growing up gay in a straight man's world" *The Velvet Rage*, because he'd found that so many of his gay patients were suppressing a "deep and abiding anger that results from growing up in an environment when I learn that who I am as a gay person is unacceptable, perhaps even unlovable."[1] This unacknowledged rage distorted their psyches and drove them to behavior that was destructive not only to themselves but to others.

As gay Christians begin to acknowledge the ways they were taught to worship a god who didn't love them, an abuser god, they may discover deep layers of anger, pain, grief, and confusion.

If this is what you're feeling, the best I can tell you is that this is normal and you can come through it. God will not abandon you because you're angry at the people who first taught you to know him.

In fact, God in his justice judges the way you were mistreated and mistaught more severely than you ever could. Luke and Matthew both quote Jesus saying, "Whoever causes one of these little ones who believe in me to sin, it would be better for him to have a great millstone hung around his neck and to be drowned in the depths of the sea" (Mt 18:6). Anyone who taught you that gay people can't enter the Kingdom of God, that you have no future in the Church and no hope in heaven unless you become straight, sinned against you and caused you to sin. They taught you to hate yourself and to believe in the false, abuser god. Jesus' own words pronounce a judgment on them that is terrifying. And you may need to spend some time with that terrifying judgment. You may need to let it sink in. Let it comfort you; let it shield you from the homophobia you were taught.

Psalm 23, that great psalm of comfort which begins, "The Lord is my shepherd," tells us that a good shepherd offers refuge and restoration, and his guidance of the sheep is always accompanied by protection. The Lord promises to welcome those whom others reject ("You set a table before me / in front of my enemies"). Those who take on the responsibility of guiding their flock *without* cherishing and protecting them are among the "enemies" this psalm rebukes. Part of the comfort the good shepherd offers is this rebuke to bad shepherds, who, far from laying down their lives for the sheep, expected the sheep to obey without receiving protection or care.

This is a betrayal. If you discover "a deep and abiding anger" within you, the core of that anger may be grief. You may be mourning terrible losses: the loss of your family's love and comfort, the loss of friends, the loss of your church's support. These people told you, *We will always be there for you. We love you. God loves you.* But then when you came out, or they found out that you were gay, it turned out that this promise had always had a caveat. There was always a condition. They were never who they said they were.

That's heartbreaking. That's a kind of death: the death of your hopes for them, your belief that they might be what they promised to be. It *may* be possible to reestablish a relationship with the people they turned out to be—but first you may need to acknowledge to yourself that you are grieving. You are mourning the loss of the people you thought they were. You're mourning the loss of the people they should have been.

Chris Damian is a gay Catholic who writes about both his acceptance of Church teaching and the anger he's had to grapple with because of his mistreatment by fellow Christians. In one searing post, he writes:

> I thought back to a conversation I had had with a close Catholic friend who was struggling to relate to my life as a gay man.
>
> "I'm sorry," the friend had said. "This has all been really hard for me. I've spent the last few weeks racking my brain trying to figure this all out. I don't know how to resolve these things."
>
> It was a tense time in my life, and also in our relationship. I wanted to scream back at him spitefully. I wanted to yell. I felt within me something coming up, something deep inside that I have had to bear for many years.
>
> But I didn't yell. If you yell, then you're emotional, you're not rational, you're letting your feelings get the best of you. I shut those things down, just as I have so many other things in of the course of my life. I said calmly, "Well now you know how I've felt my whole life. And it's hard, to be honest, to feel compassion for what you're experiencing because what you're feeling now is what I've had to go through every day." It seems to me a luxury that he was experiencing this for the first time, and largely vicariously.
>
> He had gone to me for an answer, or perhaps for permission. Should he back away from me and my life? He wanted permission to stop showing up at the events of my life, about which he now had moral confusion. Things like celebrations of my relationship, dinners with my partner's parents, the coming commitment ceremony.

But I would not give it to him. I would not tell him what to do, or tell him that what I thought he was doing was ok, that I thought it was right and just. I would not lie to him, and I would not give him permission to hurt me. If he decided to hurt me it would be his decision, not mine. I would not walk away. I would not back down. I held out my hand with the invitation, and I would not retract it to make him more comfortable, so that he could sidestep the issue that is my life. . . .

I do not owe them my explanation. For a gay man to offer his ecclesial community something other than anger is to go beyond the realm of justice. They are not entitled to an explanation. *We* are entitled to empathy. For them to give us empathy would be an exercise of justice. But for us to give an explanation would be an exercise of *mercy*.

They are not entitled to our words. But at times we give, because they are poor. I write something down and put it out for them, because I want to live in a world of mercy, and the only choice I have in bringing about such a world is whether *I* will offer mercy. For a gay man to share his experiences with the Church is to offer an impoverished Church mercy.[2]

Jesus judges those who harmed you; he also cherishes them. As Chris writes above, God asks us to go beyond justice and into mercy, while not forgetting what justice demands.

If we carefully control and never express any anger or impatience, the people around us will have much less chance to understand us and give us what we need. But there's an obvious danger in expressing our anger as well. We might fear, *What if I start to be honest about what I'm feeling and the rage overwhelms me? What if it never stops? What if it changes me into someone I don't want to become?*

In asserting the truth that you aren't uniquely sinful *because you're gay*, you can become vulnerable to the temptations of self-righteousness. It can become tempting to assert that you are a good sheep after all. You are the good one and all those contra-cepting, adulterous straight people are the bad ones. Or you are the good one and all those judgmental, cruel Christians are the bad ones. There's even scriptural warrant for this, it seems: Jesus sums up the parable of the Pharisee and the publican by saying that the publican (a tax collector, collaborating with the oppressive Roman government) "went home justified" (Lk 18:14), while the hyper-devout Pharisee did not.

But notice that the publican *doesn't* pray, "I thank God that my sins are not as the sins of this judgmental, hypocritical Pharisee." He doesn't exalt himself for being so very humble. He doesn't give in to the temptation to meta-pharisaism: judging others for how they've sinned in judging you.

Gay people can act ugly when their suppressed shame and fear begin to transform into rage. Rage and self-righteousness can be the waste products of the process of transforming misery into honesty, and it's tempting to dump all of those toxic byproducts onto your family or your friends. This will not make you feel better in the long term. In general if you have to dump all that fury somewhere, God can take it; God will still be there, unchanged and unsurprised, when you're spent. No matter how long it takes. No matter what you do or where you go while the gusts of rage are battering your boat.[3]

Anger and Forgiveness

If you grew up Christian, you were probably taught that forgiveness is a Christian duty. Or maybe you were taught the far less truthful secular idea that forgiveness is necessary for your mental health, that it's a form of psychic hygiene to "let go" of anger or blame.

For a long time I wondered what forgiveness really *meant*. What was I supposed to do, in order to forgive someone? Did I have to make myself feel differently about them—was that even possible? Did I have to act as if they'd never done anything wrong? Eventually I settled on the idea that I had to in some way seek their good, whether that meant helping them with things they needed or simply praying for them.

Now I wonder if a deeper understanding of forgiveness is grounded in honesty. We make an honest reckoning of the harm done us—even when the people who hurt us are also people who love us and who gave us a great deal. And then we reckon equally honestly with our own total dependence on God. We've needed forgiveness from God and also from other people: for things we remember and regret, but also for things we don't remember and things we still haven't realized were wrong.

We forgive because we have been forgiven ourselves by God. This linkage is made explicit in the Lord's Prayer (forgive us our debts, *as* we forgive those indebted to us), and it means that every time we forgive, we confirm our trust that God has forgiven us.

Once more we return to the central problem of this book: by making it hard for gay people to trust God, our churches have made it brutally hard for us to live out Christian ethics. The common sufferings discussed in the "Gay Christian Drinking Game" make chastity hard; they also make forgiveness hard. Gay Christians often find it hard to trust that we ourselves are entirely forgiven by a God whose strength and tenderness will never abandon us, no matter what we do. And so we try to forgive others without having first *known* what it is to be forgiven.

Many gay people, especially those who were raised Christian, feel pressure to forgive too quickly. The pressure to forgive can become a pressure toward dishonesty—toward pretending that others didn't really hurt you that badly. Especially when the people who hurt you most are also people you love, you can be tempted to rush past an honest reckoning of the harm they did to you and to your understanding of God. Knowing their good intentions, knowing their love for you, you force your eyes away from the harms. You think that this willed ignorance is humility. And then you're surprised when you start to reckon with your real experiences and discover a huge, seething mass of rage.

God does call us to forgive those who harmed us. This doesn't mean you necessarily have to speak to them. There are times when you have to express forgiveness in your prayers for them and in trying to live with compassion, rather than in ongoing contact with them.

But even with those whom you are able to keep in your life, with whom you can reconcile in person, you may need to work toward forgiveness over time. If you want to forgive, but find yourself furious and indignant instead, it may help to recognize that these painful emotions are the result of long-delayed honesty. And honesty is the necessary precursor of true, cruciform forgiveness.

Let me throw out what's maybe a weird metaphor. If you've seen *Mad Max: Fury Road*, you will remember that the title character gets kidnapped and used as an unwilling blood donor for a vicious warlord and his army. They call him a "bloodbag," and he ends up strapped to the front of a "warboy's" truck so that his blood can continue to flow into the veins of the ones who enslave him.

Later on, and I'll try not to spoil this more than necessary, Max has been rescued and has begun to build bonds of trust for the first time in his postapocalyptic life. His freedom is still full of risk and terror, and it requires of him an awful sacrifice. He chooses to give his blood—in the exact same way that it was taken from him before—in order to save a beloved comrade's life.

I choked up at this scene, not just because it's an inherently haunting image, but because it depicts a kind of recovery and sacrifice I have seen in so many gay Christian lives. Many of us spent years or even decades in an obedience, maybe in a celibacy, which was brutal and dehumanizing for us. Sometimes we were silent about what this cost us, muzzled like Max. Other times we, like Max, were strapped to the front of the Church, trying to witness to God's work in our lives or to the beauty of the Church's teaching but still getting used as weapons to attack other gay people.

Over time I've seen many people get free. Our freedom is never total, not in this life. But I've seen people learn that they are human, made in the image of God. I've watched them find comrades and make choices out of love rather than terror and shame.

And in this freedom they continue to sacrifice. They still live in obedience: working toward forgiveness, accepting celibacy. But the meaning of this self-surrender has changed utterly. Now their sacrifices are not slavery and punishment, but gift and hope.

Six

IT'S THE SODOM AND GOMORRAH SHOW! SEX, SHAME, AND HOPE

> my hips don't lie. my brother's hips can-
> not tell the truth. how will you escape our
> dungeon
> —a logic puzzle from @saraphernalia[1]

Oh, hey, we've reached the chapter about sexual sin. Bring on the dancing girls!

Lots of gay people have learned certain falsehoods about our sexual sins. There's the falsehood that gay sins are uniquely bad and shameful. Gay people who grow up in the churches are often taught that our sexual urges separate us from common humanity, making us an especially threatening or disgusting class of people. We often grow up feeling that being gay makes our sexual desire especially uncontrollable. (Maybe if we were *ever* taught good paths for our same-sex longings, the sexual aspects of those longings would be less frightening and more under our control? *Just a thought.*) We're often taught that our sins are "unnatural," whereas straight sins are just kind of wrong. What a great thing to have on your tombstone— you know, AT LEAST ALL THE EVIL HE DID WAS NORMAL.

But there's also the falsehood of lumping all gay sins together. One way of speaking about sin is that all sins are infinitely wrong because all sins are rejections of the infinite love of God. This is only one aspect of sin, and the Church recognizes another truth when she distinguishes between, for example, mortal and venial sin. I personally find the extreme "all sins are infinitely and equally bad" language comforting, since it means my sins are no worse than anyone else's. There is no one I can look down on, and no one can look down on me; I am no better than a murderer. We are all criminals, and this is the basis of our solidarity.

And yet different crimes do require different pastoral responses. Different wounds (all sin is damage) require different forms of care. Sex within a gay marriage is wrong; so is a casual hookup; so is abusing your power to pressure someone to sleep with you. But the path forward—the sacrifices God is calling you to make and the love God is calling you to experience and share—likely looks very different in these three cases. Masturbation is wrong and porn is wrong, but porn is a lot more likely to involve exploitation, and that makes a difference in how we repent, make amends, and heal.

Our churches' willingness to lump all "gay sin" together makes it harder for people to articulate the differences between abusive and respectful gay relationships and, therefore, makes it harder for people to identify love. If you don't know which things are care (even care wrongly expressed) and which are contempt or cruelty, it is harder for you to follow the God who is Love.

This chapter attempts to address people in one kind of situation: unpartnered people who feel that their sexual desires and actions are uncontrollable. This is not a chapter about the sexual sin woven into a loving, respectful, sexually faithful gay marriage. It isn't a chapter about the unique pain and harms caused by infidelity. Nor is it a chapter about the abuse of power that takes place in some forms of sexual sin.

Even for those of us who did not grow up feeling shame specific to being gay, experiences of uncontrollable or compulsive sexual urges can evoke a unique shame. If you're sinning sexually with other people (including the people who work in the porn industry), there's the added shame and sorrow for the way you're using them;

if you're sinnin' alone, with porn or without it, there's a special humiliation in the sheer isolation of this form of sexuality. And one of the cute little ironies of the spiritual life is that this intense shame over sexual misbehavior often makes it harder for us to learn chastity, not easier.

This chapter is based on my own experience of sexual sin as well as other people's. I can't present myself as an experienced guide to chastity. I suck at celibacy and always have. I can't say, "Here is my foolproof method for getting free of porn, rejecting lust, and treating your body as a temple of the Holy Spirit rather than a sleazy casino of depleting pleasures," because I have not learned to do those things myself. As I'm drafting this chapter, the last time I used porn was seven-and-a-half weeks ago (you know your life is in control when you're counting in *half* weeks), and I really hope I can drop a footnote to say that by the time the book was finished it was much longer.²

So this chapter is not primarily about moral improvement. I will talk a little bit about what has helped me to grow in chastity (I used to be worse!) and what has helped other people. But primarily, the ideas in this chapter are my best attempts to articulate some ways of looking at our sexual sins in ways that make it easier to experience God's love. This chapter in a certain sense is less about chastity and more about perseverance and trust.

That experience of God's mercy and care will often make chastity more plausible—but even if you don't end up acting better, this experience of God's love is inherently good. Getting to know God's love for you is not solely or even primarily medicine for your moral ailments. Knowing God's love for you, and learning to respond to him with love in return, is simply the purpose of your life.

You will likely have better ways of understanding your own experience, which might be inspired by some of what you find here but will be attuned to your own needs and circumstances. The best "reframings" for you will probably be the ones you discover yourself. So keep looking.

Finding Peace with Oneself

First of all, let me get this thing out of the way: this chapter isn't as distinct from the last several as it might seem. My own life in the Church has been ridiculously easy, and my upbringing left me with only carry-on baggage. So my own struggles with sexual sin were not tangled up with the harms done to me by others.

But for a lot of gay people, compulsive sexuality is a form of self-harm. That can be true even when it's also a search for communion or, you know, for fun and sexual release. Chastity is a form of integrity, a harmony between our beliefs and our actions: peace between body and soul. And lots of gay people don't feel as if we deserve peace or are capable of integrity. This feeling of worthlessness can be the result of sexual abuse, or simply the result of growing up in churches where your longings were treated as shameful barriers to relationship with God.

My friend Chris Damian (same guy I quoted in the previous chapter), in a short post that you should read in full, writes:

> I'd heard about people thinking they'd deserved their assaults. I'd always believed that such thoughts were categorically wrong. But then I understood those people, because I became one of them.
>
> I really did believe that I deserved mine, not necessarily because I did anything to invite it, but because I believed that I didn't deserve *anything*. At that time in my life, I thought that I was worthless, and that this was just what happened when you were worthless. After it happened, I just sat in my car on a secluded dark street and felt disgusting. I felt exactly how I thought I should feel. Not because what he did was disgusting, but because I thought that *I* was disgusting, and that that was why it happened to me.
>
> I think this is a great part of why the common presentation of the "Christian sexual ethic" fails to convince gay people. Because celibacy only works when you

see it as an exalted state, when you hold your sexuality close to yourself because you are convinced of its value. Only when I really see my body as something of great value do I stop treating it as merely a dispensary device for my pleasure or someone else's. Only when I think my kisses are precious do I begin to see my sexuality as priceless.

But Christians often don't make gay people *feel* valuable. They see our sexuality as a curse, rather than a gift. They often make us feel afraid, isolated, unwanted. In the Christian world, being gay is an occupational hazard, a social constraint, and an intellectual problem. We often find our lives reduced to an argument over language, or a political debate, or an "occasion for sin" (or an occasion for someone else's "complicity" in sin). Christians often struggle in a tension between seeing us as problems to be solved (with as little entanglement in those problems as possible) and seeing us as persons to be befriended (which, as in all real friendships, would involve problems not susceptible to easy or obvious "solutions," but which friends will find themselves bound up in). We often feel that Christians would rather just not deal with us and the complexities of our lives and relationships.

And when Christians don't want us, why should we want ourselves? Pope Benedict XVI once wrote, "It is only through the You that the I can come into itself." But gay people spend so much time fearing that we are not a "You" to Christians. And so we cannot come into *ourselves* as Christians. In this context, the Christian call to celibacy does not become a call to dignity, but a call to worthlessness, to unwantedness, to isolation. In this context, we have yet to experience the deep acceptance which would make celibacy a desirable *good*.[3]

After abuse, sexual assault, trauma, or other forms of suffering and injustice, compulsive sexuality can be a way of punishing yourself for suffering (or for existing, or for being gay). It can be a form of self-medication, chasing the endorphin rush of sex that brings color to a life that can seem blank and meaningless.

It can also, and this is maybe more complicated, be a way of taking back your body and your sexuality. Sex—even anonymous sex, even compulsive and depleting sex—may be something you're doing in order to prove that your body is your own and not your abuser's (and not, most painfully, the abuser god's.) It may be something you're doing in order to learn that your sexuality—including both your desires and your gay orientation—is something that can give you and other people pleasure. It's attractive, not repellent or "tolerated." If you've been mistreated and rejected because of being gay, sex can be a way of shouting, *In your face!* at those who harmed you.

And this is often a response of life and not death—kicking and fighting, not succumbing to despair. Look, *obviously* I do not think anonymous sex is the right way to "fight back" or address those who harmed you; you probably don't either. But often when we sin, we're seeking some good thing in the wrong way. The goods being sought in gay sex may include *self-respect* as well as more obvious possibilities such as longing for communion, same-sex love, ecstasy, and self-gift.[4]

In a different post, Chris writes:

> My counselor and I have spent many sessions exploring the intersections between my own pornography use and my relationship to my erotic life. One particularly helpful realization was a connection between my attachment to pornography and feelings of disassociation from my sexuality. She and I suspect this connection arose partly from internalized shame associated with my perceptions of my Catholic peers' expectations and fears about acceptance in Catholic communities.
>
> To be honest, I was skeptical of this idea at first, worried that my counselor was just blaming Church

teaching and wanting me to abandon it. But she wasn't. I
realized that these attachments to porn had much more
to do with my *fears* about some Christian communities, and with my *relationship* to Church teaching (as
opposed to the teaching itself). Currently, I'm working
on these issues by trying to be more intentional about
where I find acceptance, and also by being creative in
my approach to Church teaching, focusing on what
actually helps me to live it out, as opposed to what
everyone else thinks I should do.[5]

Chastity often requires a certain level of peace with oneself and
with God—a willingness to take care of your heart, soul, and body,
and a willingness to entrust all these aspects of yourself to God. The
shame, suspicion, falsehoods, and lack of guidance that gay people
find in too many of our churches make this peace exceptionally
hard to sustain.

Speaking with the Body

I mentioned above that sexual sin can be "about" self-respect or
anger. The exciting thing is that sex can be "about" pretty much
anything! One characteristic of contemporary American life is the
rise of sex as the language in which we articulate virtually all of
our desires and needs. It can sometimes be helpful to ask yourself
what exactly you're trying to say with this language when you have
sex, or sin sexually in other ways. What are you trying to do with
your body?

Sex can be a way of using your body to express self-loathing, as
I described above. It can be a way of reinforcing your own (false)
beliefs that you are worthless, incapable of self-control, doomed or
damned or disgusting.

It can also be a way of reminding yourself that your body is not
alien to you. Sex can be a way of reclaiming your body from abuse,
as described above, or from the alienation that so many gay people

experience because of homophobia—or from the alienation that so many human beings experience because of the Fall. Sex can be a way of learning gratitude to your body, learning to live within your own sensations and experiences rather than denying that you have them. This is true even when the sex is sinful.

Sex can be a way of speaking love, affection, forgiveness, or trust. We sometimes use sex to articulate our desire to serve and care for another person, as well as our promise to stick by them when things are hard. This is true even when the sex is sinful.

Sex can be a way of expressing anger at the churches or people who have harmed you. Acting out anger through sex is probably always wrong, but that doesn't mean the anger itself is unjustified.

Sex can be a way of seeking validation—something you probably are not receiving in a lot of other places in your life. Receiving validation of your attractiveness or desirability is powerful for anybody; for people who have faced a lot of rejection and suspicion, it's basically crack.[6]

Sex can be a way of seeking ecstasy: self-forgetting contact with someone outside the trapped narcissistic self. Sex can be a way of getting out of your own head with all its neuroses and squirrelly dishonesties. Sex can be a way of experiencing the pure white fire of contact with God's creation, dissolving into it for a moment, a reminder that we were made for bliss. It's weird how obvious it is that this is true even when the sex is sinful.

It can help immensely to find another person—ideally, a spiritual director or other mentor—who understands what you're trying to say with your sexual sins. Such a person can help you figure out what you want to say with your body and what God is calling you to say with your body. Slowly you may find other languages with which to say what is holy in your sexuality and other ways to address (by surrendering) your self-loathing.

Habits

Most of this chapter focuses on the *chastity* aspect of compulsive sexual sin. But if your sexuality has become compulsive, focusing on chastity may be the wrong approach. You may find it better to understand your problem as a bad habit like many other bad habits. We often think that we can't change our life-damaging habits until we understand why we do them—or at least until we *want* to change them. And that may be true in many cases, but my experience of quitting drinking was almost the opposite of this. To the extent that I understand what I was trying to do with alcoholic drinking, I began to gain this understanding only after I'd been sober for a few months. I don't think I started *wanting* sobriety until many months later—maybe toward the end of the first year. Nowadays it's easy to see sobriety as a blessing, but that was not true when I started.

I personally have found that I have to treat compulsive sins as basic bad habits, which are broken and replaced with better habits, using whichever standard addiction-recovery tools make sense to me. Often only after the habit has been broken have I started to discern some hints about what I used my addiction for—which spiritual needs it addressed.

Things that have helped me break compulsive sinful habits in the past include the following:

- dumb rewards that are only meaningful to me, like rereading a favorite book or watching a new movie;
- reminding myself that humiliation is good for my soul;
- finding that one priest who's a million years old and gives gentle penances without questions or advice;
- imagining fictional characters changing in the ways I want to change;
- going to bed at a set time, getting enough sleep, and then getting out of bed when my alarm goes off (which I started as a Lenten discipline and am trying to continue even after Easter, since it seems to make chastity, specifically, much easier);

- getting really interested in my problems and reading a lot about them, so that eventually I found some things that helped;
- paying more attention to my menstrual cycle (real talk);
- praying even while I was still involved in sin, which I know feels awful but honors the ambivalence Christians really feel when we're entwined with sin;
- learning that this ambivalence is a normal part of change;
- and eating nice things when I felt unhappy.

Not all of that will help you, and some of it may harm. For example, both "remember that humiliation is good for you" and "use food as a reward" are tools for some but dangers for others. Moreover, habit-formation advice often implies a degree of control over your circumstances, which may not be available to you in every aspect of your life. All these advice lists say, "For better mental health, get regular sleep," but who's gonna say, "For better spiritual health, give your employees predictable hours"?

More than any specific "technique," I want to suggest that you can think about your spiritual and moral problems in a way that makes sense to you, even if it doesn't work for or make sense to others.

What you're trying to do is to reduce the space in your life for your besetting sins. I think of this as "filling the room." In Luke 11:24–26 (and Mt 12:43–45), Jesus warns, "When an unclean spirit goes out of someone, it roams through arid regions searching for rest but, finding none, it says, 'I shall return to my home from which I came.' But upon returning, it finds it swept clean and put in order. Then it goes and brings back seven other spirits more wicked than itself who move in and dwell there, and the last condition of that man is worse than the first."

This may sound like a counsel of despair. What's the point of trying, if the demons are just going to come back even worse?

I am not a scripture scholar, so this is only a personal interpretation, but to me, this passage suggests that when the demons came back, they found the "room" of the sufferer's soul *empty*. Ready and waiting for them, cleaned but not inhabited. If you ask how you can fill the room with light (it doesn't have to be busy activity!— just the gentle light of God's love), you make it cleaner, but far less hospitable to demons.

The surrealist Rene Magritte's 1960 painting *The Tomb of the Wrestlers* depicts a small bare room with one window—but the room is entirely filled with a gigantic red rose. Where's a demon gonna live if you've filled your room with a rose?

What About When It Doesn't Work?

But the three sections above are still about *trying* to be chaste. Now we'll turn to experiencing God's love even when those strenuous efforts fail.

Impure Souls in Love

St. John Climacus, a seventh-century (*ish*; we don't know for sure) monk of the monastery on Mount Sinai, whose work is beloved especially in Orthodox and Byzantine Catholic Christianity, has a word of comfort for the sleazier types among us: "I have watched impure souls mad for physical love but turning what they knew of such love into a reason for penance and transferring that same capacity for love to the Lord." Peter Brown, in whose majestic study *The Body and Society: Men, Women and Sexual Renunciation in Early Christianity* I found that quote, interprets the saint's line as follows: "This redirection took palpable physical form in the infinitely precious gift of tears. . . . The fluidity of a temperament that blurred harsh boundaries ensured that the monks most prone to sensuality were often, so John had observed, more sensitive to others, and more gregarious, than were those harsh 'dry' souls who were more naturally inclined to chastity."[7]

One possible example with particular relevance for gay people is the monk Dorotheos. This Byzantine monk died around the year 560 AD and left behind letters in which he pours out his experiences in the monastery, including his distress when he fell in love with another monk. Dorotheos passed through this temptation and remained true to his vocation, eventually mixing the medicines for the monastery—like a living parable, in which the experience of sexual temptation, when "mixed" with the love of Jesus, makes a monk into a skilled healer who can bring mercy to others in distress.[8]

The idea that vulnerability to sexual temptation is often linked with gentleness and sensitivity to others fits with my own experience. Partly this is just because sexual temptation, and sexual sin, are often so humiliating. It can be easier to be gentle with others when I've had a painful recent reminder of my own weakness, and chastity is one area where I've received those reminders throughout my walk with Christ. When I'm finding chastity easier, I often find that my thoughts aren't taken up with Christ but with judgment of others, self-righteousness, self-pity. (These are signs that I have not filled my room with a rose, let me tell you.)

Moral behavior and self-control bring with them their own temptations: the temptation to judgment, the temptation to secure one's own respectability rather than seeking solidarity with the disgraced as Jesus did. I grew up in a left-wing household, and so I learned early on a line from the Socialist leader Eugene Debs, which has stuck with me all my life: "[W]hile there is a lower class, I am in it, and while there is a criminal element I am of it, and while there is a soul in prison, I am not free."[9] Christian poet and eminent homosexual W. H. Auden once wrote, in a letter to his friend Christopher Isherwood, "Though I believe it is sinful to be queer, it has at least saved me from becoming a pillar of the Establishment."[10] I obviously would not locate the *sin* here in simply "being queer." But I would locate one virtue—or let's say one blessing, one grace—of being queer right where Auden finds it: in our inability to think ourselves better than others or be thought better than them. In an age where gay people are increasingly respectable in the secular and progressive-religious world (though still targeted in many churches), this blessing may be especially available to those who continue to have a hard time with chastity. And knowing yourself not to be respectable, you can offer gentleness and humility to those who are "criminal" in other ways, or imprisoned by other sins.

I frequently manage to be both sleazy and self-righteous, but I'm an outlier. Many of the people I know who struggle most intensely with chastity, *and who are willing to admit this struggle to others*, are startlingly humble.[11] They're generally so aware of their own sins that the humility others see in them doesn't give them much comfort. But it is still a gift to their communities—and to themselves, although the gifts God gives us are very rarely the ones we wanted.

St. Fabiola of Rome and St. Margaret of Cortona experienced conversion of heart after sexual sin and then devoted themselves to caring for sick people in poverty. Margaret also cared for her community by speaking out against injustice. She didn't let shame over her own past silence her, but rebuked her bishop for violence and high living—twice! She lived in penance and humble service, not in complicity.

If you know you've misused the first good God gave you, your body, you may be especially willing to surrender your other goods. Those who know what it's like to not be at peace with our own bodies may be all the more desperate to make peace within the body politic.[12]

Peace

When I was quitting drinking I gave myself "permission" to worry less about lust. I don't mean I stopped caring. I always took mortal sins to Confession and I did try, in my weakness and ambivalence, to be chaste. But I had found myself often lying in bed choosing between going to the liquor store and staying here with my bad thoughts. One of those options was both gravely sinful and physically deadly, so I picked the other one. I'm not proud of that, but it taught me a hard lesson about priorities in the spiritual life.

Hyperfocus on our sexual sins can make them *harder* to surrender (or overcome, if you for some reason want more butch language). You may also be at a point where if you focus on striving for chastity, you are going to end up in despair, hating God and yourself. If that's where you are, try addressing other aspects of your spiritual life first: your prayer life, your service to others, your temper, whatever you're actually ready to examine. If last week you were a huge mess sexually and missed Sunday Mass, and this week you were a huge mess sexually but went to Mass, this week was better, you know? It's all right to think of your spiritual life as a path leading you closer to God's love step by step, rather than a switch you flip. Do what you can, not what you can't; do what you will, not what you won't.

By the time you come back to consider chastity later, when you are more at peace with yourself and with God, you will probably have a different perspective on it. Chastity will look different to you, and you will be able to approach it with more longing and more stubbornness.

Trust

Few experiences of God's mercy are as convincing as the experiences we have in failure—and that includes moral failure. When you're conscious of serious sin, if you can and you're willing to, try to remind yourself that God is still with you, still seeking you. In situations of sexual sin, pray as soon as you're willing to. A lot of the time I've kind of toggled between prayer and indulgence in lust, and while that feels sort of awful (which is probably a good sign), it often has helped me break away from lust. Even when it hasn't, it has helped me remember that I'm loved, that I am still connected to God. It has helped preserve my ambivalence.

Sin separates us from God . . . which is why God is so intense about seeking us out when we are in that condition. He is always searching for us as the bride in the Song of Songs searches for her lover, even when the watchmen (our sins) beat her. She will search for her lover until she finds him. And so God is always working, even when we think we don't want him to work. He is there in our ambivalence, in our first movements back to prayer, and in our first halting, imperfect repentances. Like the father of the prodigal son, God comes running to meet us the moment we turn away from sin, before we've even told him we're sorry.

We only have the ability to repent, to confess our sins, and to do penance through God's grace. So how could we ever think he is completely absent from our lives because we've sinned?

The Heart of Flesh

And finally—even those who haven't experienced compulsive sexual sin may feel intense shame over their sexual desires. This shame is often especially acute for gay people who grew up in the churches. It isn't necessary. *A feeling isn't a sin.* And shame will only distract you from the ways God may be using your same-sex desires to illuminate a path of love for you.

But one thing shame itself can illuminate is that being gay is an area of your life over which you have basically no control. You can pray for change and go to bad therapy and go to good therapy, but probably you will still be super gay at the end of it.

And this lack of control is a gift to you. For many high-achieving, self-controlled, virtuous and dutiful young homosexuals, the gay thing is the first thing that made them admit that they couldn't order their lives through willpower alone. If being gay were a choice, we'd learn less from it. If being gay were a choice, it

couldn't do what it has done for so many gay Christians: show us
that our power is sharply limited but God's love is limitless.

If God wants to change your sexual orientation, he is fully capable of doing that. But people who have tried to become straight by
their own effort (including prayer), or who have tried to persuade
themselves and others that they were straight, generally find that
God does not have that future for them. He has something much
better: a future of honesty, both about their sexuality and about the
limits of their control. Paul begged the Lord three times to remove
the "thorn in [his] flesh," but the Lord replied, "My grace is suffi-
cient for you, for power is made perfect in weakness" (2 Cor 12:9).
In accepting the thorn-ridden life he did not want, Paul magnified
the glory of the Lord he did want.

If you are feeling shame over being gay right now, know that
there will come a day when you are grateful to be gay. There will
be a day when you are confident that the desires that you once
thought separated you forever from God have in fact brought the
two of you closer.

The normal heart you wanted is a stony heart (see Ezekiel
36:26), which you can carve to your own specifications. He has
given you instead a heart of flesh.

seven

AMBIVALENCE

In *Motivational Interviewing, Third Edition: Helping People Change*, the authors write that ambivalence about change "is a normal human experience. In fact, it is an ordinary part of the change process, a step along the way. . . . Ambivalence is simultaneously wanting and not wanting something, or wanting both of two incompatible things. It has been human nature since the dawn of time."[1]

And yet this textbook, which guides counselors and therapists who want to help people make positive changes in their lives, notes that this normal experience can also be intensely painful: "Ambivalence can be an acutely unpleasant, aversive place to remain when the pondered choice is a psychologically significant one with potential long-term consequences. . . . Often a client would find movement in either direction more comfortable than pondering the existential dilemma of intense ambivalence."[2]

Very few gay Christians are so completely surrendered to the Church—or have had such unequivocally peaceful and fruitful experiences of her—that we have no ambivalence about our faith or our obedience. I'm unusually numb to doubts: I sin and turn away from God, but I never really doubt that the Lord is right where I left him. But even I have seen how ambivalence has manifested itself in my own experience of faith. For most gay people trying to practice the Christian sexual ethic, I'd wager that ambivalence is even more pervasive.

Ambivalence about whether we are on the right path is intensely painful, and we're often ashamed even to admit that we're experiencing it. I hope knowing that it *is the normal response* will help.

Christian obedience for gay people is frustrating, countercultural (to the point that we have virtually no models for it), painful, and often made harder by those who think they're helping. It would be bizarre if we *never* wondered whether we were really on the right track.

And I've heard many gay Christians express frustration with their ambivalence itself. They wish they could just "pick a side." But they know they can't. There are times in your life when you may be called to work through your ambivalence—or just sit with it, which is even harder. You may have to confront hard questions: *Am I really persuaded by the accounts I've been given of homosexuality and the Christian sexual ethic? Should I expect to be persuaded? If I'm not persuaded, should I still trust the Church?* And you may have to accept long-term uncertainty about the answers. This is ridiculously painful and humiliating when these answers would help you shape your future and shape how you give and receive the love we all desperately need.

To the extent that I have advice, it's simply that you can't rush this stuff. What you can do is try to love while you're in this painful place. Try to give yourself in love to God and others, so that if you do get to look back on this period of ambivalence from a future in which you've found some greater security, you can know that you did your best to love and serve even when you weren't sure how.

Our ambivalence poses challenges for the people around us too. Often gay people in the churches feel external pressure to "pick a side" as well as internal pressure: People want us to declare ourselves progressive or traditional, orthodox or dissenting. That pressure can play out even in our tiny subcommunities of gay Christians. Being pressured to take sides in a conflict where your own heart and soul are the battlefield is often dehumanizing.

This is especially true when you've already been hurt in your church and have made the difficult decision to try again, to trust again. Gay people who are coming out of the disorienting misery of a toxic and homophobic church often need havens where they can sort through their own beliefs and restore their relationship with God, rather than immediately being pressured to sign a yes/no statement that can make God's love seem like just another checklist.

The yes/no checklist approach is especially galling since acceptance of the Church's guidance isn't a switch you flip from off to on. People can be unconvinced and yet willing to wait and see if further experience as a Christian changes their perspective. They can be unconvinced—and quite vocal about it!—and yet willing to live by the Christian sexual ethic on a provisional basis. They can be unconvinced and yet willing to live by the Christian sexual ethic because it's what their church teaches.[3] People can be neither convinced nor unconvinced, but simply focusing on other things as they try to rebuild their trust in Jesus and their church. People can be aware that they aren't willing to trust their church enough to accept its sexual ethic yet, but unsure which direction they're moving in. None of these situations are sinful. All of them are part of the normal experience of people in the pews.

Too often when gay people come back to church after painful experiences, they're immediately interrogated about exactly what they believe about sex. This approach damages trust, rather than helping to restore it.

For Catholics there are, of course, truths we are given by the Church as our mother and teacher. When I was confirmed I had to affirm that I believed all that the Catholic Church believes and teaches to be true. And yet I hope we can also make a welcoming space for those who are not ready to make that affirmation—in spiritual direction, in the pews, in our coffee hours and our homes, and in those online spaces that are such common occasions of sin. Undecided people, too—in their ambivalence and with their questions, with their needs for rest and shelter—are gifts God is giving our churches.

Sometimes it takes people a long time to get themselves sorted out. They make mistakes on that path, and they put themselves into situations they wish were different, but are unwilling to change. To pick an obvious example, sometimes people get into relationships they wish were celibate but instead are an unstable mix of unhappy-but-ecstatic unchastity, ambivalent repentance, and future plans for chastity that maybe they don't talk about anymore with their partner. People walk around feeling as if they're headed to hell. After all, they're going against the teaching of their church and the guidance of their own conscience, and to remind themselves that God is merciful seems too much like presuming on his mercy. And yet they don't change. What's going on there?

Sometimes people get stuck in ambivalence because even necessary change is terrifying. Ambivalence lets you pretend that you're keeping your options open, instead of succumbing to the humiliation of traditional Christian belief.

But sometimes people get stuck in ambivalence because their situation is complex and confusing. Gay Christians, specifically, receive messages from society and church that often drastically conflict with one another. On the one hand we're encouraged to trust our gut, and we're taught that doing the right thing will *feel* right. On the other hand our churches often order gay people to mistrust our emotions, to consider ourselves more damaged than other people and less able to understand our own lives. The second approach is wrong. That doesn't make the first approach infallibly right. Sexual sin (not only for gay people!) can lead to astonishing release of long-repressed emotion. It can feel not only intensely pleasurable but intensely *right*: as if in this sexual union we've discovered some truth that was long hidden from us; as if we've come home, at last and for the first time.

There's a song by the indie band the Mountain Goats called "Broom People." It's from the autobiographical album where the singer-songwriter worked through his memories and emotions after the death of his abusive stepfather. "Broom People" is about (to oversimplify a song I love) how sex with his high-school girlfriend offered the song's narrator a haven from abuse, a sign that life could have hope and ecstasy and delight in it and not just secrets and degradation. It's a song about premarital sex: sexual sin. It's also a song about being cherished and cherishing, with an intensity so unexpected and so necessary that it's shocking.

If we can accept that straight people are not lying when they say their own sexual sins can feel that way, we may have to admit that things may feel right to us and yet not be fully right. We might do things that bring us closer to the peace and harmony God wants for us, without being completely aligned with his will. (It would be weird if that were never true—if we always switched immediately from "sin that doesn't help in any way at all" to "complete harmony with God's will." Even St. Francis got rebuked now and then!) It's a little too neat, a little too American and "doing well by doing good," to think that virtue *always* feels right and sin *always* feels wrong. Our emotions are not a moral compass; all our longings and desires point toward God, toward Love, but our emotions don't always interpret these longings with complete accuracy. There will be many times in our lives when our beliefs and our emotions are in conflict rather than harmony, and in these times love of God may *feel* as if it conflicts with love of other people, even though I believe God often finds ways to bring all our loves into harmony.

Knowing how to interpret our most intense emotions is genuinely difficult. (Uh, and by "emotions" I sometimes mean "orgasms.") When sexual sin leads to intense emotions of coming home, or at last being okay, we have a hard time interpreting that in light of our prior convictions. I would suggest that these emotions can point to some real truths. Often the intensity of the pleasure of sexual sin helps people finally admit that they're probably not gonna become straight and need to figure something else out. It can be a wake-up call about what you really want, including touch, love, and caring for others as well as, uh, "emotions." It can be a wake-up call that your previous attempts to ignore your emotions and desires weren't good for you.

Maybe you've had an experience you were taught was gravely sinful (and which was probably messy, without any kind of permanent commitment, because you've been flailing around rather than trying for abstinence-until-gay-marriage), but it made you suddenly feel as though a door had opened inside you to a future of hope and joy. It isn't my place to interpret this experience for you—to tell you how to reconcile your emotions and your convictions. This is work for you to do. For what it's worth, I believe that if in the afterglow of sexual sin you suddenly feel that there is a future of hope and joy for you even while you are gay—maybe even *because* you are gay—that feeling is a glimpse of something true.

There will be some way for you to reconcile your sexuality and your conscience; or there will be some way for you to trust that obedience to God in the midst of confusion is a blessing for you and not a punishment. But walking these paths takes time. Like everything in the spiritual life, it can take much longer than you would have believed you could bear.

It's tempting to just find some *answer*, so that you can be done with the ambivalence. Why can't you just dump the person you love? Why can't you just switch to a church that does gay marriages? But if you take one of these steps in order to forestall working through your questions and suffering, you may find that these exact same questions return later; you may find yourself even more confused and frustrated, angry and self-defeating, because you thought you were done with this. Better to take the time to work through these painful questions fully, as they arise. They may still recur from time to time—you will spend the rest of your life learning more about the life God has given you—but you'll be able to face them from a place of far greater self-acceptance and acceptance of God's will.

I will offer one other note about ambivalence, which is that in my experience—including painful personal experience—gay Christians with a "traditional" sexual ethic have a very hard time respecting our own convictions. This reflects an overall lack of self-respect.

I am ambivalent (see what I did there) about self-respect in general. I've joked that if I wrote a self-help book, it would be called *The Life-Changing Magic of Low Expectations and Limited Self-Respect*. (Instead, it's called *Tenderness*. . . . Why does God never let us do what we want?) But if you don't respect your own convictions, it will be even harder for you to live up to them. If you are seeking friendship, church community, covenant friendship, or celibate partnership, try to trust that your convictions—and your willingness to sacrifice for them, to the degree that you've got that—are strengths you can offer in each of these relationships. Try to spend time with people who, even if they don't share your convictions, at least see something admirable in your honesty and desire to follow God no matter the cost.

Sometimes our lack of respect for our own convictions comes from still believing the repressive things we were taught in childhood. We might have a sneaking suspicion that we really *are* uniquely damaged and broken, incapable of real love. We might suspect that our sexual orientation is something shameful that we're "flaunting." We might suspect that when we seek out gay community we're playing with fire, and when we rejoice in it and feel safe there we're revealing that we were never real Christians at all.

These possibilities virtually never worry me. My own troubles come from the opposite direction, and I think this is true of many gay Christians who spend a lot of time in progressive environments. (Some people get their self-respect damaged from both directions! Life is a cabaret.) Many gay Christians, on some subterranean level, think of progressive Christians as our betters. We see them as more successful, which is a great way to make yourself envious; we may also see them as less rigid, more thoughtful, braver. We can tell that many of them have found ways to give and receive love, and even if we don't believe they've found the right ways, that's cold comfort when we're still flailing around trying to find any way at all. We might even feel ashamed because we think progressive Christians are more self-respecting than we are—a Mobius strip of self-blame.

We may worry that in expressing our acceptance of the sexual ethic we believe to be given to us by God, we're being arrogant— judging others, when what we are trying to do is walk humbly with our God. Sometimes we're right to worry about that! Sometimes we're running into the fact that so many Christians have presented the Christian sexual ethic to gay people in the past with brutal callousness, so even acknowledging that we believe it to be true may dredge up painful memories for ourselves or the people we talk to.

Look, it's good to regard everyone as your betters. (Yes, I read *The Imitation of Christ* like once a year, does it show?) And if you have to pick between looking down on progressive Christians because their sexual ethic is wrong and thinking they're just better people than us, the former is worse. Holding correct beliefs doesn't make anybody special. The demons themselves have a whole bunch of correct beliefs (see, e.g., Mark 3:11; Luke 4:34, 41; and James 2:19).

But downplaying the importance and goodness of Christian orthodoxy isn't humility. And treating your own conscience as a liability or an embarrassment is bad for all your relationships, including with God and even with those progressive Christians. All we can do is try to receive both our churches' teachings and the wild variety of people whom God brings into our lives with humility and gratitude. Those other people are often making the same effort with us.

eight

LOVE'S BEEN A LITTLE BIT HARD ON ME

There's a mock Christian motivational poster I saw once that bears the cheery slogan, GOD HAS A BEAUTIFUL PLAN FOR YOUR LIFE!— above a painting of Roman martyrs in the arena.

Suffering has been a part of Christian life since at least Christ's agony in the garden of Gethsemane—if not the promise to Mary that "a sword will pierce" her (see Luke 2:35). There are three principal ways I've seen the suffering of gay people, specifically, misused by Christians. Each of these misunderstandings of our suffering contains a real insight (maybe more than one!). You can accept the rough grain of insight while still thinking the mass built up around it is more of a clod than a pearl.

The Litany of Trauma

The first misuse is one with which I suspect most of you are already familiar: the litany of trauma that gay people experience, when it's used not as a rallying cry but as a warning. Gay people have higher rates of mental illness and addiction and suicide, we are more likely to experience various forms of abuse, and instead of causing nice straight Christians to say, "Oh, wow, God must really want us to cherish and fight for these people!" the lesson they draw is too often, "Okay, deffo don't be gay; got it."

The litany of trauma does evoke a kind of pity—but not the kind that leads you to listen to the people you pity, or trust what they tell you. It may even encourage mistrust and suspicion of gay people, leading Christians to treat us as if our own accounts of our lives are too damaged by trauma and mental illness to be believed. Christians are encouraged to treat straight experts (of a certain stripe) as trustworthy guides to gay people's needs and experiences, whereas our own analyses come pre-discredited.

The litany of trauma typically conflates *being gay* with "the gay lifestyle," by which Christians mean gay sex. I don't even want to hammer on this point too much, since the litany of trauma leads Christians to mistreat gay people who are in fact in sexual partnerships; it would be tacky, as well as callous and lacking in solidarity, to argue that we the celibate don't deserve this pitying scorn but maybe others do. If any gay people deserve this treatment, we do, since I'd be startled if celibate gay people were spared these traumas. The "Gay Christian Drinking Game" gives material for plenty of entertaining mental-health problems. My point is that in the litany of traumas, obedient gay Christians don't even exist—our traumas are invisible, our need for justice is ignored, and our solidarity with other gay people is suspect.

Most important, the litany of traumas offers no vision for a gay person's *future* in the Church. Its purpose is to say, "Mamas, don't let your babies grow up to be gay boys." I have never seen it deployed to argue that Christians have a special responsibility to listen to and humbly serve this suffering community.

Never, I mean, except by two groups: progressives who reject the Christian sexual ethic, and gay Christians ourselves.

The kernel of truth here is simply that many of the statistics deployed against us are true. For example, lesbian, gay, and bisexual young people are more likely to contemplate and to attempt suicide than their heterosexual peers.[1] It may be worth noting here that religious faith is correlated with lower suicidality in most American demographics—but not gay people, where placing great importance on their faith may *increase* suicidality.[2]

The statistics are right that we're vulnerable. Mistreatment by others increases that vulnerability. (Why wouldn't it?) Feeling that there's no place for us in church increases our vulnerability.

Today many Christians cite John 8:3–11 to remind us that Jesus told the woman caught in adultery not to sin anymore. But that is the *last* thing that happens in Jesus' interaction with her. The *first* thing Jesus does is to unsettle the crowd of people who want to stone her; then he defends her; then he tells her that he does not condemn her. Only once she is safe does he speak of her sin and the need for a new way of life.

Gay kids who grow up in the churches often feel as if people are gathering stones before they've even had a chance to do the adultery—before they even know what their desires might mean. The scary statistics reflect that experience of being unsheltered: given morality without protection. Jesus' priorities, in which people are protected first and *then* guided, are, of course, the better way.

Nothing But a Cross

The second misuse of suffering is the idea that gay people (sorry, "people struggling with same-sex attraction") are given "our cross" in order to bring us closer to Christ. We've even been encouraged to think of ourselves as "victim souls," singled out for special suffering that we can offer for others. Weirdly, if you then say that this experience has given you particular insights into Christian life, you're accused of narcissism for "thinking you're special." The *only* gift you're allowed to give straight people is your suffering! If it's a cross, why can't I learn from it? Why can't I rejoice and glory in it?

Defining gayness as solely a source of suffering or a cross to bear misrepresents many people's experiences and makes it harder for gay Christians to see the joys, beauties, and communities available to us because of our sexual orientation. It also misrepresents *straight* experience. I don't know that my experience of my sexuality is any more of a "cross" than some of my straight friends' experience of theirs. There are certain forms of suffering that are more common among gay Christians, and not all of them are the result of injustice. I'll discuss them toward the end of this chapter. I hope we can be honest about these common forms of suffering without defining all people's experience of being gay as, primarily, a cross.

Often the association of same-sex attraction with suffering is used to argue that we shouldn't accept ourselves as gay; we shouldn't seek out the good aspects of gay experience; and we should assume that our lives will be lonely deserts with *only* Jesus for company, instead of seeking to bind ourselves to others.

I enjoy being gay. I love the communities my experience has given me; I love spending time with other gay people, especially other gay Christians. I love the insights this marginal, outsider experience offers—the queer perspective on contemporary American and Christian life. I love noticing and attending to the beauty of women. The world is full of beautiful ladies! What a joy. What a gift to notice it.

Each of these delights comes with challenges. Solidarity is hard, and I have made a lot of mistakes in trying to live it out. The outsider experience is intellectually and spiritually fruitful but also confusing and uncomfortable, full of temptations to despair and to pride. Attentiveness to women's beauty can become lustful objectification instead of delighted and self-abandoned gratitude. But the challenges and failures don't define the experience.

Being gay, for me, has been a tapestry woven more with light than with shadow. That's luck, not virtue on my part ("No joke," my confessors sigh), but at least it indicates that identifying gayness with victimhood is unnecessary. I believe this identification can also be harmful when it's imposed on us by well-meaning straight Christians, because it can lead us to ignore the good things God is showering into our lives—including the good things God is offering us precisely in our experience of being gay.

But there are truths hidden in this misunderstanding of our suffering too. Suffering *does* bring us closer to Christ, or at least it can. Voluntarily taking on suffering or embracing with gratitude the suffering that comes to us in life are normal and good ways to imitate Christ. In the desert our souls can blossom. Willing acceptance of suffering, especially when accompanied by devotion to the crucified Lord and his blessed wounds, can bring peace, humility, and even sweetness and joy to the Christian soul.

I say that, but the truth is, I'm lousy at accepting suffering—I'm more in tune with Daffy Duck's lament: "I'm not like other people. I can't stand pain. It hurts me." But I've seen the fruits in my own life of embracing humiliation, being grateful for painful experiences, and contemplating the wounded and suffering Savior.

None of this was connected to my sexual orientation. (It is connected to my alcoholism and recovery, but not to being gay, at least as far as I can tell.) For other people this spirituality of humiliation and grateful acceptance of suffering does have some connection to their experience of being gay. When actual gay/same-sex attracted people identify their own experience of sexuality as a "cross," they're often expressing insights into their spiritual lives and touching on deep truths. They aren't misusing suffering—as long as they don't argue that being gay can *only* be a cross.

I love the gory Spanish crucifixes with bloodied, grimy knees, the devotion to our Lord precisely in his humiliation and suffering, and I might not have come into the Church without it. But I've also noticed that many people who were abused or oppressed by other Christians desperately need a Christian spirituality that acknowledges that suffering is *bad*, that Jesus came to free us from our misery, that obedience to him is liberation, and that Jesus wants for us joy and delight and love unending.

The Cross is our life; the Cross is an obscenity. Jesus willingly yielded himself to the Cross; Jesus triumphed on the Cross to conquer death, sin, Satan, and all the powers of this world. Christian wisdom holds both of these truths at once, knowing that some Christian paths will emphasize surrender and some liberation.

And as a final note on this subject, I'd caution the gay humiliophile not to assume that all our suffering is inevitable. A lot of it is injustice that we have a duty to oppose. The experiences itemized in the "Gay Christian Drinking Game" *didn't have to happen*. These sufferings aren't inherent in being gay; they aren't inherent in desiring illicit sex; they aren't inherent in being drawn toward disordered expressions of love as well as ordered ones. You can shelter yourself in the wounds of Christ without making excuses for the centurion who pierced him!

You can welcome humiliation, seek Christ in your loneliness, and be grateful for your chance at some tiny share of his suffering, while still seeking justice and compassion for your gay brethren.

But Have You Tried Not Suffering?

These previous two misuses of gay suffering come mostly from what I guess we have to call the "conservative" side of our current disputes. The third misuse of suffering comes from the "progressive" side, and it's rooted in a misunderstanding of what our suffering means. Many times I've heard progressives—or people considering a progressive sexual ethic—argue that the Christian sexual ethic can't be justified, because it causes so much suffering to gay people.

It's obvious that *many* gay people suffer immensely in trying to live up to their church's sexual ethic. And the truth being expressed in this progressive misunderstanding of our suffering is that gay suffering is often an invisible hand writing in huge red letters on the walls of our souls: SOMETHING NEEDS TO CHANGE.

Moreover, what needs to change might be our churches. In my opinion, a huge amount of gay suffering is caused by the churches' unwillingness to recognize and honor same-sex love. It's one thing to give up sex and very much another to give up love, devotion, commitment, and sharing your life with someone. The loss of models of same-sex love harms all gay Christians, including those who have no interest in covenant friendship or celibate partnership. It makes us fear our longings; it makes straight Christians suspicious of all our friendships.

Probably even more of gay people's suffering in the churches is caused by churches' desire to brand being gay as sinful in itself. When churches pressure us to change something that God has given us no means to change, of course the suffering that results will be unbearable. These are aspects of gay people's suffering that point out catastrophic failures of Christian fidelity and witness on the part of our churches. In these areas, the progressive critique is pointing at a serious problem: gay people suffer because the churches need to change.

But I don't want to assume that everybody's suffering is explained solely by the aspects of church culture that I already think are awful. I don't think I can honestly argue that in the hoped-for future toward which this book is working—where our churches have remembered the scriptural models of same-sex love and where gay people are welcomed rather than shamed—the Christian sexual ethic won't make anybody miserable. Knowing that you won't experience the form of sexual union for which you long is always going to be desperately painful for some people. If you fall in love, that love will be expressed in a covenant friendship or celibate partnership rather than in sacramental marriage. Even in a culture that doesn't idolize marriage the way ours does, knowing that your covenant won't be a sacrament may be very painful. The limits the Church actually sets are hard, even if they're not nearly as hard as the limits within which our local pharisees have caged us.

What about when our suffering causes individual gay believers to reassess our spiritual lives? This is the other side of the coin from the previous chapter's discussion of pleasure in sin. Does suffering mean we're on the wrong path?

Here too we see the truth contained in the progressive argument, because, yes, sometimes our suffering does mean that we need to make some changes. Many of the people I quote in this book only noticed the untruths they'd been taught about God, and God's relationship to gay people, because their suffering became so great that they were willing to reconsider the Christianity they'd grown up with (or accepted on conversion). It's just *true* that we need a new understanding of chastity, if our old understanding of chastity was one in which same-sex love or gay people had no place. It's just *true* that we need a new understanding of the place of morality, if we previously related to the Christian ethic as a rulebook God consults to see how close or far we are from him, rather than a response to God's cherishing and unstoppable love. If we've been taught to have faith in Jesus the abusive boyfriend (see chapter 4), it's just *true* that we need to discover Jesus the Good Shepherd. Suffering can be an indication that we have neglected these truths.

As we begin to realize how much of our suffering was unnecessary, how much of it was always the result of societal injustice that warped not only our spiritual life but the souls of the people who inflicted it on us, this realization may change our whole hermeneutic (the principles by which we interpret scripture and Church teaching). That hermeneutic can change in a bunch of ways, some good, some not so good.

We may start to judge scriptural interpretation or practical spiritual guidance on the basis of whether it makes us *feel* worse or better, more despairing or more hopeful. In the caricature version, you "KonMari" your religion, throwing out any aspects of the Christian faith that don't "spark joy." A more charitable interpretation would be that people often desperately need to find a form of Christianity that doesn't make them want to kill themselves. The experience of Christ's love is often so good! So sweet and beautiful. He is so wonderful to love and be loved by. Why would anyone think the path to him would lead through so much pain?

The problem is simply that suffering on its own is not a means of determining a Christian ethic. This becomes obvious once you talk to people who have experienced many forms of unbearable suffering. It isn't that hard to find people for whom the prospect of carrying a baby to term was terrifying, overwhelming, unbearable. That does not mean we have the right to take the life of an unborn child.

It isn't that hard to find people for whom forgiveness is unbearable. When you're in that situation you need support and shelter from other Christians; you need to have your trauma acknowledged and your anger heard. You need justice in this life if you can get it, and confidence in God's justice if you can't. You might need to wait until you are safe, or until the person who abused you is dead and buried, before you can forgive. You need patience with yourself; trust that God can give you the grace to do what seems impossible; acceptance that nobody knows when or how you'll be freed to forgive; and confidence that God loves you right now, before that time has come. The alternative of saying that forgiveness isn't *really* a Christian duty, that we can hate our enemies if loving them is too hard, that Jesus didn't really mean it—that helps nobody.

It isn't that hard to find people for whom, because of the trauma they'd experienced at the hands of Christians, simply praying or considering the possibility that Christ is Lord is unbearably painful. Still Christians need to pray (or work toward healing enough that they can pray); still Christ is Lord.

We are told that we will have to take up our own crosses (Mt 16:24, Lk 9:23). We're told to bear one another's burdens (Gal 6:2), which suggests that some of these burdens will be too heavy for one person to carry alone. We're promised persecution several times, even in the comforting verse of Mark 10:30. We're promised that those who suffer for the Gospel are *blessed* (Mt 5:3–12)—not that they're repressed or self-hating. And we are not promised that we'll get to choose how we suffer or what we sacrifice. We don't know what God will ask, but it likely won't be what we expected and it likely won't be what we want.

As far as this question of the meaning of our suffering affects individual gay Christians' practices, rather than our beliefs, I don't know that I can say more than what I said in *Gay and Catholic.* Sometimes you will have to pick up your cross. Suffering isn't always a sign that you're doing something wrong: Jesus wasn't doing anything wrong in Gethsemane when he sweated blood. You don't have to feel ashamed of your struggles—they don't mean you're being a bad Christian; they don't mean that God has forgotten you; and they don't mean that you aren't working hard enough or loving God enough. But if all of that sounds like more than you can bear right now, *that's also all right.* God is thrilled by every movement you make toward him, even if you are not living completely in harmony with your conscience on sexual ethics (or if you're unsure what your conscience calls you to).

And beyond all of that, there's one urgent truth that for some people will be the overridingly important point: God doesn't want you to kill yourself.[3]

If you have experienced terrible suffering because of the way you were taught Christianity, your spiritual journey will require discovering the worth of your own life and the depth of God's tenderness toward you. These new experiences will reshape how you understand the truths of the faith that you were taught.

So does that mean you'll embrace a progressive sexual ethic? Girl, that is up to you—or, I should say, that is dependent on what *you* believe to be true. Your ethics are not determined by your suffering. Do as much as you currently can of what you believe to be right. When you don't do what you believe to be right, do your best to be honest about the conflict between your convictions and your actions. In the long run this is better for your self-respect than pretending you believe something you don't quite.

God is not out to get you. His mercy is for you. He who promised us a cross promised us also the bliss of eternal life with God.

He who promised us persecution and suffering for the sake of the Gospel promised us also restoration and homecoming, to the mansions of our Father. Our suffering and our sacrifices have as their purpose communion with the God who has always cherished us. If your Christianity isn't grounded in these truths—then, yes, something needs to change.

It isn't always obvious which suffering we should stay with and which we should try to relieve. Where suffering is the result of injustice, of others' mistreatment of you, often it's best not primarily for your sake but for theirs to be honest about what their actions cost you. Where suffering manifests as self-loathing, it is a rejection of God's act of creating and sustaining you; it's a denial that you are made in God's image. Loathing the *imago Dei* is a pretty intense form of blasphemy, and you shouldn't do it to anybody, *even* yourself. (When you are your own worst enemy, love your enemy, you know?) These forms of suffering don't necessarily need to be endured without complaint or any attempt at change, and thinking of self-loathing as the martyr's crown God has prepared for you is a good way to damage yourself and the people around you. But these distinctions are imperfect guides to the nature of suffering. There is no foolproof handbook for what you should do when you suffer.

All of that is true for everybody. But there are ways in which Christians often speak about suffering that are especially unhelpful to gay Christians.

I once visited a Catholic school where one teacher had posted up homemade signs in his classroom: YOUR LIFE HAS A PURPOSE. THIS PURPOSE IS HAPPINESS. HAPPINESS COMES FROM VIRTUE.

That school was actually working hard to be both orthodox and welcoming, to be gentle and to delight in its LGBT students. No shade to that Catholic school! But it's wild to me that so much Catholic discussion of morality argues *both* that doing the right thing will make you happy *and* that our culture has strayed far from the Gospel. Do those things really go together? When virtue is unsupported, even penalized, by the surrounding culture, *it feels worse!* It's harder! It hurts![4]

Nonconformity can bring its own forms of happiness: camaraderie, for example. The hard lessons a countercultural life teaches give rise to hard-won, deeply appreciated joys. But at the end of the day, if the path God has marked out for you is countercultural, it will also be difficult. The happiness you receive on that path, which is real and which I hope I've illustrated in this book, will be mixed with a lot of suffering that will come to you *because* you're trying to give your life to God.

For a Christian, being gay closes off certain options we might intensely want. These are experiences of helplessness that, when accepted, can become surrender—but surrender hurts. The ascetic surrender of our own shockingly intense wants, which is part of the witness and beauty of celibacy described in chapter 3, typically comes with a whole lot of unbeautiful feelings.

For gay Christians one of the most common forms of suffering is anxiety about the future, or the fear that there is no future for us that we want. Why should you live alone or at others' mercy while your friends pair off? Why should you be turned down by a religious order? Why should you do the hard work of coming out, of coming to terms with your sexuality and continuing to practice your faith (or returning to the practice of your faith), and still be left at sea, with no harbor for your love in sight? *And, hey*, you may say, *I know we're supposed to pretend that being gay is just about love and pretty feelings, but I can't imagine how I will manage to live a life without sexual union. Why on earth do I have to do it?*

These are hard questions, but in an individual life they may not be the most urgent questions. *Why me?* is rarely an answerable question. (Why *not* you? Why should other people suffer, but not you?) Even the simpler *why*, which maybe you do need to ask and wrestle with, more readily prompts blame or cheap theodicy than communion with God. You may need to ask, instead, how you can experience God's mercy and gentleness within experiences of suffering and anxiety. Sometimes that will look like entering into Christ's suffering through the door of your own. Sometimes that idea just makes you angry.

Telling yourself, "You just need to trust God more!" is only slightly less infuriating (and maybe slightly more damaging) than being told that by other, well-meaning Christians. But it can sometimes help to seek out a "spiritual vocabulary" that illuminates the kind of trust you need, for the kind of person you are. Our languages for the spiritual life bear widely varying connotations and assumptions and speak to different audiences. Jean Pierre de Caussade's *Abandonment to Divine Providence* and Henri Nouwen's *Return of the Prodigal Son* speak very different languages and address very different needs. To radically oversimplify, de Caussade is speaking to people who need to learn that they're not in control; they can be as weird as the wild diversity of the saints and still conform their lives to Christ. Nouwen is speaking to people who need to learn that they're cherished. And yet the result of the Caussadian *abandoning myself to God's providence* looks a lot like the Nouwenish *becoming confident that I am God's beloved*. Both books describe a process of learning to trust that God is Love.

Maybe the first step for you in trusting God is trusting that there will be a language out there for your anguish and your needs—and if there isn't one already, you can put one together from whatever you are able to say and know. And to break that first step down into an even more manageable piece, one thing you might do is simply keep a record of everything you read, hear, or see that in some way resonates with you. What makes sense in the midst of chaos? Then you may be able to apply each of these small things to new questions, remote from the ones that first made them ring true to you. Or you might not! In which case you move on and wait for another small thing to make sense.

There's no pressure here. People may tell you that you need to trust God faster. Christians do this to everybody, but I think many feel extra anxiety about the open expression of suffering or mistrust by gay Christians, sometimes because they reflexively judge our faith as disingenuous and sometimes because our suffering makes them feel guilty. The people who pressure you to resolve your ambivalence on a schedule that makes faith more comfortable for *them* usually mean you need to feel better faster . . . which in turn just means they think you should smile more. Not necessary.

Of course all this busy advice of mine is thrown into shadow by the Cross. As St. John Henry Newman preached, "The management of our hearts is quite above us."[5]

Often our suffering is compounded by feeling that God is absent or far away. At the moment when we most desperately want the comfort of feeling God's presence, we feel only absence. This is the cry from the Cross: "My God, my God, why have you forsaken me?"

The longer I live as a Christian, the more I notice the theme of waiting and longing in scripture. *Waiting* is a key image of celibacy: the bride, in her bedchamber, waits in solitude for her bridegroom to come to her—for that consummation of which we can only receive hints and glimpses in this lifetime.

Israel must wait, through the long years of exile, for the Messiah and simply for home. The disciples must wait until the Resurrection before they understand much of what Jesus taught them. (Which must've been hard, since they can't even make it through a single hour in Gethsemane!) At Jesus' Ascension he promises to send us a comforter, the Holy Spirit. Much of our lives feel as if they're spent in the nine days between Ascension and Pentecost. Most of our lives are *promise*—which is to say, most of our lives are desert.

Psalm 130 is often used in prayers for the dead. It begins in loss and anguish and attains, not to fulfillment or redemption, but to hope:

> Out of the depths I call to you, Lord;
>   Lord, hear my cry! . . .
> I wait for the Lord,
>   my soul waits

and I hope for his word.
My soul looks for the Lord
   more than sentinels for daybreak.
More than sentinels for daybreak,
   let Israel hope in the LORD. . . .
And he will redeem Israel
   from all its sins. (Ps 130:1–2a, 5–7a, 8)

Part IV

HOW TO KNOW GOD'S TENDERNESS

Yes, we have reached the final section of the book—hurrah! The hard part is over. This fourth section explores specific habits and prayer practices that may help you to experience God's tenderness. I hope these suggestions provoke you to shape your own practices, since you'll know your own needs better than I do.

Let's begin with a big one—an adventure, a long journey that begins with two short words.

nine

COME OUT, COME OUT, WHEREVER YOU ARE!

Look, I will say what every responsible homosexual says: many people have good reasons not to come out. If you're closeted because you fear for your physical safety, because you're economically dependent on people who will reject you if they know you're gay, or for any other reason you find compelling, it is not my place to say, "Come out anyway!"

But I will say two things. The first is that as I was preparing to write this book I asked LGBT people with "a traditional sexual ethic" about what helped them experience God's tenderness, and *by far* the most common answer was, "The people who were good to me when I came out."

The more terrified you are, in your secret heart, that because you're gay God does not really love or cherish you, the more you may need to see that tender love on the face of someone who knows your orientation and welcomes you.

When you come out, you may lose friends. You may lose family. You may lose *a lot*. But the people you do not lose—or the new people you meet, who know you as you are and love you *for it*, not in spite of it—are the people who will show you who Jesus is.

And the second thing I'll say is that coming out is not a switch you flip from off to on. If you are not able to be open in your current circumstances, you may be able to reach out anonymously online (my email is eve_tushnet@yahoo.com, and I know other trustworthy people who can talk to you). Online is a real place, too, and your actions there can have uncontrollable consequences just as all our actions may, so you should be *very* cautious with your trust. But it may be possible to experience that welcoming gaze without risking your job, your safety, or your relationships.

Gregg Webb, a gay Orthodox Christian, wrote this about the lessons of his first ten years out of the closet:

> The closet allowed me to believe fundamental lies about myself and my relationship with others. The closet told me that I was un-loveable and that my shame and self-hate was justified. In the silence of my closet I believed the lies that I told myself, and the echo chamber of my fear was deafening. When someone told me, "I love you" I knew they couldn't really mean it. They couldn't mean it because they didn't know that I was gay. I believed that nobody could love me because I was gay, so therefore their love was contingent upon my secret being secret. Most of these lies had no basis in reality, but in the closet you can easily mistake shadows for monsters. Everything becomes distorted in the dim light and you believe that outside the closet is scarier than the darkness you've surrounded yourself with.
>
> Reading over old journals I'm still shocked by my outlook on friendships. I often found myself writing letters to unknown friends that would never be shared. Letters that were filled with fear, shame, and an overwhelming sense that to continue loving me, even after knowing the horror of my desires[,] would be a great feat of grace. I truly believed that my sexual orientation, my constant attraction and emotional interest in my own sex, was cause for rejection. It made me a leper, someone only the bravest could continue to associate with. My fears were almost entirely unproven[,] and as I began the difficult process of self-disclosure, I came to see just how baseless my beliefs were.
>
> In every case, without exception, disclosing my sexual orientation was the beginning of vulnerability and greater levels of intimacy and friendship. "I love you,"

was no longer contingent on a but, and slowly became a fact that could sink into my being. Slowly I was able to believe that I was lovable by friends and family even as a gay man. This began opening the possibility for me to actually believe and know that God loves me. The same fear, shame and rejection I projected on the most important relationships around me, I also projected onto God. The problem was that I could never escape from God. There was no coming out to Him, only the constant terror that my darkest shame was already known to Him. It was only by soaking in the enduring love of those around me, that the same doubts and fears I projected onto my relationship with God could also begin to fade.

The closet is a cold, dark, vicious lie told by the devil to keep us away from God and from the love of those around us. Sadly, a few do not have my story and still face a significant possibility of rejection after coming out. Their fear of being abandoned because of their orientation is justified and can often [become] reality after coming out. Circumstances may truly require some to remain in the closet. However, everyone deserves to be fully loved by at least someone. Even if only a few people know your secret, it only takes a few dissenting voices to begin countering the lies about your worth. Through their love, the love of God may also slowly sink into your being and became manifest.[1]

The last time I checked this post, there was one comment. It's not a response everyone will be able to get, even though everyone should. It was this: "Wow, it's been ten years! Thanks for sharing that with the world. I love you!!! Mom."

Let me close this section by noting that many of you were never able to conceal your orientation completely. Before you even knew why, other people clocked you for gay and punished you for it. In coming out, you transform their suspicions and their labeling into your honesty. God, like the people who harmed you, has always known the ways in which you fit other people's ideas of "gay," both inside and out. But God has always known you *in order to* love you.

ten

ADMIRE A HOMOSEXUAL FOR JESUS

This brings me to my next suggestion—which is something you can do without coming out, though coming out often makes it easier: get to know gay people.

Much of the advice gay Christians have received in the past from pastors and other mentors served to separate us from other gay people. We were encouraged to fear friendships with other gay people, or participation in gay communities. Priests, ministers, and counselors viewed gay people primarily as sources of sexual temptation, not much-needed mentors; gay communities were treated as temptations—to promiscuity at best, heresy at worst.[1]

If you get to know gay people in contexts likely to bring out their virtues (so, not the club scene), you will start to admire at least a few of them. This is huge. The more you have been taught that gay people are inherently narcissistic, the more you need to know gay people who pour out their lives in selfless service. The more you've been taught that gay people are immature, the more you need to know gay people who are eerily stable and responsible. The more you've been taught that gay people are difficult to love—so that even tolerating us is asking a lot—the more you need to know gay people, so you can discover how easily you will love us. (Some of us, but enough of us.)

When I went to the Revoice conference in 2018—as far as I know, the very first conference for LGBT and same-sex attracted

Christians who hold a "traditional" sexual ethic—my icebreaker question for everybody was, "What's been the best part of the conference for you so far?" And every person said one of two things. Either they named the worship, or they simply said, "The people." For the first time in our lives (it was the first time in *my* life, and being gay and Catholic is literally my job) we were surrounded by hundreds of other LGBT/same-sex attracted people who shared our convictions. One of the reasons the worship was so moving is that we were a crowd of people who had often been at best invisible in our churches, at worst rejected and targeted, but who now gathered together to praise Jesus openly, hiding nothing, welcomed by other people as we have always been welcomed by the Lord.

For the entire conference I was holding myself back from caterwauling, "I love everybody in this baaaaaaaaaaar!" I was among my people, for the first time, and my people turned out to be easy to love.

But I don't only mean that you might benefit from knowing other gay Christians who share your sexual ethic. That's an amazing experience and irreplaceable, of course. When I became Catholic, I didn't even know *of* any other gay person who had actually tried to live in harmony with Church teaching. Being alone like that led me to flail around, wasting time and hurting myself and others. But I'm talking here about the benefits that can come from knowing LGBT people in general. Having friends or heroes who *don't* share your sexual ethic can even bring unique comforts—it can help you understand, in your bones, that you don't earn love by your obedience and that your life and your faith are not defined by your sexual ethic. There's great joy in knowing and loving your basic gay person, who has left the Catholic sexual ethic far behind if he or she ever shared it.

There are a lot of other things, too, of course. Remember the "Gay Christian Drinking Game"? That stuff leaves its marks on people. Communities of people who have grown up isolated and afraid, separated even from their own families by secrets they don't know how to understand or accept, are communities of wounded people. I mean, find me a community that isn't. But I do think gay people's painful formative experiences make community-building both more urgent and, sometimes, harder.

So my point about getting to know gay people and gay communities is not, "Come on in! The water's fine!" That's always a false advertisement for human communities and a setup for betrayal and disappointment. It's more that if you get to know other gay people, you will almost certainly love some of us—and that will shift your understanding of who *you* are, in all your most difficult aspects. (At the very least, it'll pinpoint your problems more accurately: "Oh, I'm not a sleazebag because I'm *gay*. I'm a sleazebag because I act like a homosexual Graham Greene hero. I wonder why I do that.")

Jesus loves us and loves spending time with us. And you want to be like Jesus, no?

Knowing and Loving Gay Christians

I mentioned the Revoice conference. You can find the conference online at http://revoice.us, and there are scholarships available to help you make it there. There are also online communities, including Eden Invitation, which offers book clubs and forums for same-sex attracted Catholics. If you email me (my email is still eve_tushnet@yahoo.com, as it was in the last chapter), I will tell you what I know about other possible communities, where people pray together, laugh together, argue together (there is no online community without drama), and share their daily triumphs and sorrows. Online community may not be *as* real as speaking face-to-face, in the flesh; but it can be real enough to save your life or guide you. And some online communities also have IRL meetups, like a miniature Revoice, across the United States and in a few other countries.

Your nearest city may have a center for LGBT people; if not, many universities and colleges have LGBT student groups.

One way of getting to know and love gay people is to serve them, and as of the writing of this book I can recommend the Trevor Project as a potential place to serve. The Trevor Project runs a twenty-four–hour suicide-prevention hotline for LGBTQ young people. Obviously that kind of work isn't right for everyone. But if you're in a place where you can do it and want to do it, it's a chance to offer immediate crisis care to people regardless of their sexual ethic or religious faith. You'll be asked to listen and to offer one unshakable conviction: that LGBT people's lives are infinitely precious.

As you stand with other gay people, you are likely to find it easier to believe that God stands with you—that God is for you, and not against you. And this confidence that the Cross defeats the powers of this world will help you work for justice and for peace. James H. Cone's study of black American Christianity's resistance to injustice, *The Cross and the Lynching Tree*, quotes a black woman participant in the civil rights movement: "We stood up," she says. "Me and God stood up."[2]

eleven

LEAD, KINDLY LIGHT

When I edited *Christ's Body, Christ's Wounds* (the anthology with the "Jesus Is Not an Abusive Boyfriend" essay from chapter 4), I discovered that many stories of holding on to faith after trauma had one thing in common: the intervention of a gentle and trustworthy priest.

Guidance is something gay Christians often need with special intensity—and yet we face extra barriers to finding this guidance. We're trying to live a way of life with virtually no models in the public life of our churches, let alone the broader society. And when we turn to authority figures in our churches for help, we often encounter misunderstanding and suspicion. We need shepherds. How do we find good ones?

I asked a group of LGBT "Side B"[1] Christians how they'd found spiritual directors (aka spiritual fathers or mothers, mentors, guides) and therapists whom they could trust. The first thing many of them said was that they were blunt and explained up front, in the first meeting, that they had no interest in ex-gay approaches *or* approaches that would try to get them to accept gay marriage and ditch their church's teachings. Putting yourself out there, facing the awkwardness right at the beginning, and trusting your gut will weed out a lot of people who could do damage to you later. (This may be especially important if you are in a covenant friendship or celibate partnership—you don't want to be guided by someone who will try to break you two up just because you're the same sex.) And even as your relationship with your spiritual director or therapist proceeds, keep in mind that it's always okay to seek a different guide if you're getting harmful advice based on misinformation or bad theology. Others' misunderstandings are facts about them, not a reflection of your relationship with God.

Be aware that some therapists will say that they don't do "ex-gay" or "reparative" therapy, but will still approach you with the assumption that the goal of therapy is to make you straight. If they're reducing all your problems to your sexuality, or trying to shove you into narrow psychoanalytic categories (for example, telling you things about your family background or gender identity that don't seem to fit), they are likely not a good match for you. Some good questions to ask yourself are: *Does this person believe that there's a good future for me as a gay person, not just as a hypothetical future straight person? Is this therapist or spiritual guide helping me to love Jesus and accept myself as I am now, or are self-acceptance and moving forward in my life constantly being delayed until my sexuality is "fixed"?*

A couple of people said that the best way is always to get a personal referral from someone you trust; this is yet another thing that will be easier if you're able to get to know gay people who share your convictions. One woman noted that she had to give up on "Christian therapists" entirely and find a secular therapist who was nonetheless willing to accept her convictions and help her live them out.

These are serious challenges. And yet if you can find someone to help you sort through your nonsense and bring it all to Christ, someone who can encourage you in prayer and find the paths of love in what can seem like a vast, empty wilderness, you will get a hint of the love of Christ the Gentle Shepherd. The Good Shepherd doesn't abandon or harm his sheep; he protects them, guides them home when they're lost, and walks alongside them when the path is rocky.

twelve

ASK DIFFERENT QUESTIONS

When I became Catholic, I thought a Catholic lesbian was supposed to do two things: (1) don't date girls and (2) think real hard about the theological basis for the Church's sexual ethic. I am . . . not great at the first thing, and also not great at the second thing. Fortunately it turns out that the way my culture (including the Catholic culture) trained me to think about the intersection of my faith and sexuality was not the only or the best way.

The questions our churches expect us to ask, or prompt us to ask, are often good questions: "How can I avoid sexual sin?" is a good question for a Christian to ask herself. But they are rarely the best questions. They're often good questions that, when posed in isolation, prompt bad answers. If you ask how to avoid sexual sin, but never ask how to pour yourself out in love or how to avoid despair and self-hatred, you will probably make bad choices that lead you away from Christ's love.

Gay Christians spend years wrestling with the wrong questions. One way of getting to know the God who is Love, as a gay person, is to change the questions you ask about God's role in your life. You don't have to be trapped in the old, tormenting, wide-awake-at-three-a.m. questions. (*Lord, do you love me? Why am I like this? Will I be alone forever? Is this because my parents divorced? Am I lying to myself when I think it's okay to be gay? Do you hate me? Is the thing you call love the same as the thing normal people call hate?*) Instead, you can ask questions meant to illuminate the ways God is loving you, right now.

So, for example, you can ask: *How has my experience of being gay revealed Christ working in my life?*

Where is Christ revealing himself to you in the confusion? In the perseverance with which you obey, doggedly pulling in the traces, even when you don't understand why? In the perseverance with which you've sought justice? In others' beauty, in others' care, in others' acceptance? In the humiliation, in the community and friendships, in the ways you've had to—and been able to—see your church from the outside?

If you're having a hard time seeing Christ in your gay experience, try thinking about aspects of your spiritual life that don't immediately seem relevant. What in your faith already resonates with you—favorite scripture passages, devotions, saints, vocabularies like "abandonment to divine providence," even broader concepts like "mystery" or "rescue"?

If you want to be cheesy and "journal about it," a practice I highly recommend, you might try making a list of five or six touchstones of this kind: a hymn, an image, a quotation, a moment in the life of Christ. Then go through each of them and imagine a fellow gay Christian, who shares your convictions, saying, "That's my favorite too! It really helps me understand what God is doing with my sexuality." What might that person mean? What would your sexuality look like through the lenses of these aspects of the faith that you already love?

thirteen

A WALKING CHURCH

When we worship God in church, our whole being is embraced. The liturgy—the ritual by which we worship—touches our senses. We're surrounded by song and prayer, by images of Christ and the saints, maybe by the smells of incense and candle wax. There are also distractions, all our little Martha concerns, but these distractions now take place in the context of the liturgy, and the liturgy recollects us when we get too caught up in thoughts or practical worries.

And then we leave the church, and we are quickly surrounded by noisy liturgies honoring very different gods. Unlike Jesus, these other gods aren't attainable by everybody. They're gods for whose favor we must compete; they're gods who promise success and threaten failure. These are the gods of fame, wealth, a fulfilling job, economic security, as well as the gods of sex, romance, marriage, family.

I don't mean to say that fulfilling work or family are bad things. I mean to say that our society has made them idols to be worshipped, rather than gifts to be accepted when and as God brings them. Poetry and reason are basically good, but Apollo is a false god. Love and sex are basically good, but Aphrodite is a distortion of their meaning. And every trip to the supermarket plunges you into a temple to false gods: the magazine covers about celebrities, or about how to lose weight and attract a man, or about political messianism and political hatreds; the pop songs, in which love without sexual pleasure is simply unimaginable.

If you want to go to the movies, how many of your choices will show characters whose lives are shaped by love of God? By contrast, how many are about finding romantic success?

The limited vision of love presented by our surroundings confines our own imaginations and makes it harder for celibate people to imagine how we might love. This limited vision of love makes it harder for us to take God's love seriously, as real love. It makes it somewhat harder for everyone, even married people, to see friendship and community as real love, though these loves are less marginalized than love of God. (I have a pet theory that one reason for the current crazes for superheroes on the big screen, and procedurals on TV, is that these are stories of "found family": stories in which the most important interpersonal relationships are *not* romantic, but communal and dedicated to service.)

Look, as a gay person you will have your nose rubbed in a lot of the hard aspects of Christian life—not least the difficulty of loving other Christians. If you don't make an effort, you're likely to fall into patterns where your "Christian life" is strenuous and full of uncertainty, whereas your life "in the world" is a relief. Your secular life will be full of images of hope and love, which may make you envious or fill you with longing but at least seem *real*. Your worldly life will start to feel natural and your Christian life artificial or forced.

One way to think about this problem and address it is to create a "liturgy" for yourself, in resistance to the false gods, that you can live within wherever you go. It's been startling to me how the whole atmosphere of my life changes when I am punctuating my day with set prayers, listening to music where God's love is real, and reading books about real or fictional Catholics. The less "churchy" this stuff is, the better (in some ways)—especially if church has been a source of pain for you. You can seek out artistic expressions of God's love that feel very different from your painful memories.

Maybe that means a movie about monks loving their Muslim neighbors and confronting the possibility of martyrdom (2010's *Of Gods and Men*). Maybe it means a Swedish film about tween punker girls in early-eighties Stockholm and their quietly rebellious Christian bandmate (2013's *We Are the Best!*). I don't restrict myself to these stories or this music, but I do seek them out; they won't just fall into my lap the way superhero stories will.

An everyday life set to the rhythms of prayer, adorned with stories and images of lives in which God's love is the most vital love there is, is life in a different genre. It's a way of stepping out of the kinds of stories your culture expects you to believe—stories that make us anxious consumers, insatiably hungry for love and respect—and into the kinds of stories you actually do believe. It's a way of living as who you are.

fourteen

BEING OF SERVICE

There's a famous quotation, often attributed to Mother Teresa, although I don't know that that's reliable:

> The fruit of silence is prayer.
> The fruit of prayer is faith.
> The fruit of faith is love.
> The fruit of love is service.
> The fruit of service is peace.

This final idea, that service brings peace, is incorporated into the practice of Alcoholics Anonymous. In AA people in the early stages of recovery are given small, imaginable things to do, such as filling the coffee maker, to get them through the huge, unimaginable transition to sobriety. If your life with Christ seems unimaginable, if you're deeply conflicted or unhappy, one thing you might try is being of service to others.

There are three obvious ways to approach service. One is to look for the small, undeniable things: the empty coffee makers of the suffering world. If you are making sandwiches with your church's homeless ministry—or making soup to serve in a park with the anarchist group Food Not Bombs (like, you don't have to tie yourself to your church if you don't want to)—you are putting something unquestionably good out into the world. If a floor is swept because you swept it, or a person eats something tasty because you made it with care, you can be pretty sure that you are doing *something* God wants you to do. This is very Mr. Rogers but, hey, we live in an age of painful earnestness, so: when you smile at someone who needs to be seen and welcomed, you are fulfilling at least a part of your purpose in this world.

The second way to approach service is to ask yourself what your life lacks, and figure out if there's a way to receive it while serving others. This is part of how I ended up in crisis pregnancy counseling, which I've done once a week for the past fifteen years and which has been both anchor and compass in my often-wandering spiritual life. I knew I needed to be of service to women. If I wasn't going to do that in a same-sex marriage, then I needed to find somewhere else; the pregnancy center provided a women's community where I could serve.[1]

One need a lot of celibate people aren't sure how to fill is our need to be fruitful. We have a need and, I think, a calling, to serve the next generation. That may be why so many gay people I know are teachers or volunteer with children.

> Steve Yoder: For nearly five years, I've been volunteering at a local hospital that primarily serves children. I started volunteering there because I knew that I enjoy working with children and that children respond well to me, and also because friends whose children had been in this hospital had shared their positive experiences with me. The hospital understandably has a vigorous screening and training process for new volunteers, but once I started volunteering I quickly realized what a gift this opportunity was for me. In a typical week, I go to the hospital for a couple hours one evening after my office job ends, and I walk through the units knocking on patients' doors and offering to play with them. What we do is

up to the patient—we might play Uno, watch a movie, color pictures, or just talk. And when there's a need, I might hold a baby who's crying and talk or sing to her until she calms down and falls asleep. Each of these children is uniquely beautiful in his own way, but they're generally alone for most of their time in the hospital because their parents have jobs to work or other children to tend to. The most important thing is simply to be present to each of them and let them know they're loved, and my celibacy lets me be present to them in a way that I probably couldn't if I had a spouse and children of my own. And what the children give back to me is a blessing—the simple joy of spending time together, gratitude for many gifts I so often take for granted, inspiration from the children's example of resilience, and a much saner perspective on the challenges I face in my own life.[2]

You can also just go to your friends who have kids and get to know them better. We have this weird cultural script nowadays that says people separate themselves from their single, childless friends when they marry and have kids. There are real pressures pushing people with children away from those without, but honestly, your friends still want to see you. They're just tired! They have new things to share with you—and new people. If you are looking for a way to serve both the next generation and your own, be there to babysit your friends' kids.

I've been lucky enough to be an "auntie" for my best friend's children. When she had her first, I realized that it was harder for her to find time to yap on the phone or write long emails, so I decided I'd visit her as often as I could. I go up to see her now maybe once a month to every other month, for about five days at a time. This isn't something everybody could do, obviously, but you may have friends closer to home who would appreciate just as much somebody making the extra effort to be with them and their kids.

The third way to think about being of service is to put yourself in situations where you will have to tell other people what you most need to hear yourself. I know gay, celibate people who have worked with at-risk teenagers, for example. Telling them that God loves them or that their lives have value no matter what they've done or how they feel is also a way of telling yourself that. Being present for someone else unconditionally can make it a little more believable that God is present for you in the same way.

Intercessory prayer is also a form of service. This is when you pray for other people's needs: *Please, Lord, bless [my cousin, those who have harmed me, gay teens] and help them know your love.* This is a service you can perform even when other acts of service aren't available to you. But I've focused on practical Martha-type tasks here because prayer can sometimes get you tangled up in your own head, and the point here is to get you out of your head—and especially to help you stop thinking about your sexuality.

Even if your decision to put yourself more at others' service is the result of thinking about your sexuality, most forms of service won't focus on issues of faith and sexuality. The more confused or entangled you are in these concerns, the more you need ways of living out your faith that distract you from them.

The fact that you're reading this book suggests that some portion of your life is taken up with wrestling with questions of faith and sexuality. Perhaps the subtlest, most Screwtape-y danger of this wrestling is that it will take up too much of your time, too much of your mind, too much of your soul. Literally any spiritual practice that *isn't* thinking about or praying about your sexuality will help you avoid this danger.

fifteen

2 FAST 2 FABULOUS

Is this not, rather, the fast that I choose:
releasing those bound unjustly,
untying the thongs of the yoke;
Setting free the oppressed,
breaking off every yoke?
—Isaiah 58:6

Fasting is such a hallowed and beloved Christian practice that over the ages saints have attributed to it every possible spiritual purpose. St. Basil the Great wrote that fasting "is a safeguard of a soul, a stabilizing companion to the body, a weapon for the brave, a discipline for champions."[1] It's good for the weak *and* for the strong! It's a floor wax *and* a dessert topping![2]

Fasting is good for gay Christians because it's good for all Christians. But let me suggest a specific way to think about your fasting—and other acts of asceticism—which may be especially relevant to you as you deepen your experience of God's love. Fasting is willingly forgoing a good thing in order to share the suffering of others and, ultimately, the suffering of Christ. It is a deprivation which is not a punishment. In this way it may serve as a reminder of what you're hoping the other deprivations and surrendered desires in your life may become.

As you begin to explore the possibility that God is better and gentler than you had imagined, it's good to have this reminder that we are still called to bear our own crosses—and to bear one another's burdens. Fasting is our regular reminder that, as Eamon Duffy puts it, "to be Christian is to stand among the needy."[3] In our

161

desperate searches and spiritual struggles, fasting can ground us in the reality that others also have struggles and needs, and we can serve them even when we aren't sure where God will ultimately lead us.

And in a life that is often characterized by confusion and longing, it is good to have a reminder that all fasts alternate with feasts. One of the five zillion purposes of fasting is, in fact, to prepare us for these feasts and, ultimately, for the heavenly wedding feast with the Bridegroom, Christ.

So here are a few questions to ask yourself, as you seek to know God's tenderness: *How can I learn to fast in gratitude for Christ's sacrifice, not as a form of self-punishment? How can I learn to fast in solidarity with the Body of Christ, not as someone singled out as uniquely sinful* or *someone solely absorbed in my own problems? Who and what can help me trust that fasting is only for a season, whereas feasting, at the wedding feast of the Lamb, is what God has prepared for me?*

sixteen

IT'S HIS BODY AND I'LL CRY IF I WANT TO

There's a (mostly) Catholic practice called eucharistic adoration, which has certain features I think many gay Christians will appreciate. Catholics believe that the bread and wine brought to the altar are transformed into the Body and Blood of Christ at the consecration, and so Christ is fully present in the Eucharist we eat during Mass. But you can adore Christ in the Eucharist even outside of the Mass. Often nowadays this adoration will take place when the Eucharist is "exposed" (visible) to the faithful in a fancy setting called a monstrance, but you can do adoration when the Eucharist is enclosed in the tabernacle as well. Anyway, this section is not about adoration as such, but about some characteristics of adoration that have made it so fruitful in my life and that may be worth seeking out in the practices of your own church.

The thing about adoration is you don't have to do anything. You don't need a "guide to eucharistic adoration," as you might use for Confession, because the only step is to show up. All you have to do is be with Jesus. You can sit with Jesus, you can kneel before Jesus, you can argue with Jesus, you can yell at Jesus (in your mind, I mean, since there will be other people there too), or you can cry with or near or even *at* Jesus. Few things are as traditional as angry crying at adoration. In eucharistic adoration I encounter Jesus' Body, at once exposed and reserved, as the body of the celibate is at once exposed to temptation, ridicule, suffering, and reserved from the most obvious form of union. He comes to be a gift to me, and I don't have to do anything at all except spend some time in his presence.

Adoration tends to have less of a social or communal vibe than Mass. The Mass is a shared feast in which we are called to open our hearts to one another as well as to Christ. The sign or kiss of peace is one of many signals that at Mass the Body of Christ worships *together*, forgiving one another, seeking peace with one another.

But there may be times in your life in the Church when it's precisely that communal aspect of the liturgy that makes it so painful. There may be times when churchgoing makes you feel scrutinized, when you've been harmed by people there and you're angry and bitter, when you are not sure whether you can forgive and how much peace you can really share, and you are exhausted with the effort of loving your enemies in the place where you seek God's friendship. At those times adoration or similar practices of devotion may offer a refuge where you can, if I can be frank, ignore everybody else and attend solely to the Lord. You can be Mary listening at Jesus' feet, not Martha worrying about everybody else's opinions and needs.

Adoration is low-expectation. There are no prayers you're supposed to say, so you are not going to get it wrong. There are no times when you will be asked to say, "Alleluia!" when you feel heartbroken, or to ask for God's pardon when you're feeling allergic to the whole concept of guilt and sin. You can say what's on your heart, or you can be completely silent. You don't have to worry about whether you're in a position to receive Communion; you can worship the Eucharist exactly like everyone else there, no matter what condition your soul is in.[1]

If adoration just makes you anxious, or you hate it for any other reason, you don't have to do it. It's anything but obligatory. And regardless of whether eucharistic adoration, specifically, is one of your own church's practices, any way of being present to Christ without expectations will be well-suited to the times when you're most stressed, angry, or unsure. In those times you may especially need a way—any way—to adore Jesus without set prayers, without a need to force yourself to share peace with your fellow Christians, in a way that fits your own convictions.

seventeen

ALL THE NAMES OF GOD

Throughout St. Augustine's *Confessions* he addresses God directly—as "you" or as "Lord," both of which are familiar to us from the first prayers we were taught. But Augustine also calls God by other names, ardent and tender names: "Beauty," for example, or "Joy."

These are aspects of God that we may start to forget, especially if our relationship with God becomes troubled or overly abstract. God might start to seem like a distant and forbidding judge, or a disappointed parent, or just a set of harsh laws designed to make everybody a criminal. He might start to seem like just a word—not *the* Word, just *a* word, hollowed of meaning by constant repetition. "God" might start to seem like just another word for our ideas about God.

For others, the names for God that we were taught growing up carry all the baggage of the falsehoods we're trying to shed. For many gay Christians, addressing God in the terms they heard in church only calls up painful memories, doubts, anxieties, and fears of rejection. Too many of our churches have made even the name "Jesus," the Name above all names, into a weapon against gay people.

If this is your situation, it's all the more urgent to give yourself the freedom to explore other names for the One who loves you— the One who is Love.

I've heard gay Christians suggest names like "Elder Brother" or "Wonderful Counselor" (see Isaiah 9:5). Cistercian and Benedictine authors, including St. Bernard, St. Aelred, St. Anselm, and St. Gertrude the Great, plus others like St. Catherine of Siena and Julian of Norwich, spoke of Jesus or God as our soul's mother, who gives birth to our soul and nurtures us at the breast of the Crucified. At its most lyrical this imagery of Jesus as mother emphasizes our Lord's vulnerability: He is the Rock, but "the cleft rock," and "wounds have been made in his limbs, holes in the wall of his body, in which, like a dove, you may hide while you kiss them one by one."[1]

Imagery of God as Father may also disclose more of his tenderness to us if we contemplate it in a new way. The gay, celibate Episcopalian priest Wesley Hill, in his book *The Lord's Prayer: A Guide to Praying to Our Father*, writes that he often prays beneath a print of Rembrandt's painting of the return of the prodigal son. This painting emphasizes the father's gentleness, the urgency with which he presses his son to himself. Wes writes: "It's taken a couple of years for me to realize how much looking at this print hanging over my kneeler has affected the way I pray, too. In particular, I think, it's changed the way I pray the Lord's Prayer." And this change came about because the painting changed Wes's idea of who God is, which is also the central concern of the book you're holding right now. Looking into the eyes of the gentle father in Rembrandt's painting, and realizing that this is an image of *our* Father, Wes has discovered, as he writes:

> To pray for *this* Father's kingdom to come and *this* Father's will to be done is to pray for a reign of mercy, kindness, humility, and profligate divine generosity. It is to pray that debts would be remitted, rebellion ended with homecoming, and banquets held for the dissolute and the self-righteous alike. . . .
>
> To praise the kingship, the dominion, and the splendor of *this* Father is to praise the kingship of humility, the noncoercive dominion of nurturing love, and the radiant splendor of stooping and touching and embracing. To praise *this* Father "for ever and ever" is to acknowledge that such self-giving divine love is the fount of creation and redemption in eternity past and

will be the theme of the lost son's songs into eternity
future.[2]

So consider new ways to speak with God. Consider praying to
Jesus as your Friend; see how happily he comes to be with you, like
a friend grinning when she sees your nickname on her caller ID.
See how faithfully Jesus returns to you and seeks you out, searches
for you, hopes for you. He sees you in all your sordid little self-de-
ceptions and still gives everything to possess you—*rejoicing* in you,
as in that great hymn of trust, "The King of Love My Shepherd Is."

God is Beauty, who made all the beauties that pierce our hearts,
from the burning autumn moon in rags of black cloud to the laughter of the woman you love. He does not want you to reject beauty.
The beauties God has made can remind your intellect of, and prepare your heart to encounter, their Creator. He is beauty's climax
and crescendo.

I've used a couple of different methods to remind myself of who
God has been in my life. One is to add praise to my usual prayers
of petition and thanksgiving. I pray when I get up and before I go
to bed. For a while these were fairly standard recovering-alcohol-
ic-type prayers: In the morning I'd thank God for giving me this
day, I'd ask for help in the areas where I often struggle, and I'd call to
mind anything that might be especially challenging that day and ask
for help and guidance there. At night I'd (distractedly, having stayed
up too late *chez* Internet) thank God for the day that had passed
and for any "daily reprieves" I'd received from my besetting sins, try
to do a quick assessment of and apology for any sins I committed,
and ask God to bless various people in my life. That's all fine, but
these are prayers somewhat trapped in my own anxieties; they're
constrained by the daily life I already lead, and they tend to draw
my mind toward myself and other people, rather than toward God.

So I started making sure I took at least a moment to praise God.
That often meant identifying specific things the Lord had done for
me. In recovery you have the obvious gift of your daily, undeserved
sobriety. *Oh, God, you saved me when I was going down into the pit;*

you have set my feet on a rock, you have brought me refuge. There is also, always, as long as you have breath, the fact that God has preserved your life. No matter what other people think of you, God has said, by sustaining you through another day, that he wishes for you to continue to exist. A simple statement of what he has done can be a powerful prayer and an endearment. With these statements I often picture myself resting against Jesus' or the Father's breast. *You know me and you love me, my Mercy.*

God is Refuge, Rock, Redeemer; my hope, my delight, my only good; guide of my life, my only peace, my advocate, my shelter. Scripture shows God as your trustworthy Lover, your steadfast Friend. Name him for what you need most.

Name him as whatever you feel your life most painfully lacks: *Jesus, my Faith, hear me. Jesus, my father and mother, I trust in you. Jesus, my wisdom, peace, and sanity, I place my life in your hands. Jesus, my health and shelter, be with me.* He is your home, your forgiveness, your sobriety, your fearlessness.

Naming him in this way is likely to be painful and not too spiritually fruitful if you expect it to make you *feel* his presence in these aspects of your life—in general, any time you hope a prayer will make you feel something, you'll probably be disappointed. But if you make it an invitation to Jesus to enter your life through its wounds, as you enter his life through his, it can draw you close to him. If you make this kind of prayer as a statement of your willingness to encounter Christ where he seems most absent, that act of willingness in itself is one of the greatest "Acts of Faith" (the name of a standard Catholic prayer) you could make.

Consider the prayers you already say—prayers that can sometimes seem as if they've been worn down to nothingness, like those old coins where the faces have rubbed off from a century of grabby handling. I've sometimes taken a moment to go through a familiar prayer and reunderstand it, scraping off the words to expose the divine love they describe. *The Lord is with thee* becomes "Love has come to you." *Blessed is the fruit of thy womb, Jesus* becomes "You are bringing Love to a world that needs it desperately, and Love will be glad to come to us."

The familiar doxology (short hymn of praise), *For thine is the kingdom, the power, and the glory, now and forever*, can prompt reflection. *The kingdom* recalls God's sovereignty in my life, his wisdom, and my own need for his guidance in my relationships with others. *The power* reminds me that all things are in God's hands and not my own, and although I am incapable of bringing order to my life, God can restore what I mishandle or destroy. *The glory* shows me the beauty of his creation, the beauty that shines forth in every physical object and body in spite of our attempts to see only ugliness, loss, or threat.

You'll know best which prayers already speak to you. Try spending a day praying everything you already pray with an extra attentiveness to God's tenderness. What would these words mean if they meant that God cherishes you?

And seek out traditional prayers that name God in ways that help you know his love. Our traditional devotions are there to expose aspects of Christ that we would not be able to come up with on our own. Poking your nose around in a basic book of traditional prayers, or in a hymnal, book of spirituals, or other collection of expressions of our love and longing for God, may truffle up a prayer you didn't know you needed. I love the Anima Christi, a fourteenth-century prayer whose composer is uncertain:

> Soul of Christ, sanctify me.
> Body of Christ, save me.
> Blood of Christ, inebriate me.
> Water from the side of Christ, wash me.
> Passion of Christ, strengthen me.
> Good Jesus, hear me.
> In thy wounds, hide me.
> Let me not be separated from thee.
> From the malicious Enemy defend me.

At the hour of my death call me, and bid me come
    unto thee, that I may praise thee with thy saints and
    with thy angels forevermore.

I mean, look at this thing! It's a swooning, love-drunk song of joy and urgent need. It's insistently physical. The *body* of the Lord is present in this prayer, pulsing with the life he longs to give us. As someone who finds it easy to love the Church as the Bride of Christ—my conversion was, in a way, falling in love with her—I am glad to have this prayer to express my love for Jesus the man. It's good, I think (this is speculation, a personal opinion), for our prayer lives to connect us in some way to the opposite sex, especially if we are unmarried. This may be why so many priests have a special devotion to Our Lady. If nothing else, connecting with the opposite sex in prayer keeps us from feeling like the other sex is simply alien to us. We are a part of one another in the Body of Christ, even outside of the "one-flesh union" of marriage. I spend much of my life loving and serving women. It's good to have this prayer that plunges me into sexual difference, in which I long for communion with a Man. (Boy, that capital letter makes it a lot easier to long for, I gotta say.)

I love this prayer's attentiveness to Jesus' woundedness. He is open to us; he calls us to enter into his body through the sacred wounds. His wounds are open mouths, witnessing to all that his people suffer (including all that we suffer from one another). His wounds are shelters, enclosing us like the velvet curtain of the confessional, making a place where we can be utterly honest with him. His wounds are how we recognize him, like Thomas the apostle. His wounds are to be kissed and to be displayed, not to be healed—which may complicate our own desires for healing, or for change.

Ah, every line of this prayer is so wise. Look at how we ask Christ's Passion—his endurance, his suffering—to strengthen us. For Christians passion is an action. To endure without despair requires strength. And the strength it requires is not ours. We don't generate it from within. It is given to us by God. Only through Christ can we offer our own suffering in union with his.

Blood of Christ, inebriate me. From the very beginning of what people in recovery call "my drinking career," I drank like an alcoholic. I drank to get drunk. I have never seen the point of the other kind of drinking, nice drinking. I drank for ecstasy, for fearlessness, for shattering of the self and for adventure. I ended up, obviously, terrified and trapped, avoiding friends, walking that tightening barbed-wire circuit from my apartment to the liquor store, day after day.

The Anima Christi honors the desires I sought to fulfill in drinking and recalls me to the wine that gives life. The Blood of Christ gives fearlessness that lasts. It brings a self-forgetting that leads not to isolation but to deeper communion with others, and especially with God. In this prayer I beg to be drunk again, utterly given over, reeling under the influence of love and salvation.

This is the drunkenness of a lover who wants the night to last forever, who wants to remain always clasped in the beloved's arms. *Hear me,* let me speak to you. *Hide me,* hold me close, protect our intimacy, make a world for us two. *Defend me* from all who would keep us apart. *Let me not be separated from Thee*: marry me—do more than marry me; married lovers are parted at death, and for us death is only the entrance into even more complete union. At death *bid me* come to you, call me and I'll come, and I'll spend my endless days showering you with every endearment. In being with you and praising you is my delight. Let it never end.

ACKNOWLEDGMENTS

Even more than *Gay and Catholic*, this book is an attempt to honor and give voice to the communities of gay Christians who have taught me so much and sheltered me so well. So above all I thank everyone who shared their story with me, either formally in the interviews I did for this book or simply as friends share with one another. The communities associated with "Side B" and Revoice, as well as my own church's ministry Always God's Children, have been especially important to me, and I'm deeply grateful for their honesty and witness to the love and challenge of the Lord. I hope I have returned some of the pleasure and comfort I received from them.

I talked over several of the ideas here with or showed the manuscript to Gabriel Blanchard, Chris Damian, Darby DeJarnette, Aurora Griffin, Bridget Eileen Rivera, and Tommy Tighe. A conversation with Darren Calhoun also helped guide my thinking for part of the "Ambivalence" chapter. All these people's comments helped me immensely. That doesn't mean they share my beliefs—in fact, sometimes it was precisely their differences from my beliefs that allowed them to correct my thinking. Everyone who knows me knows that I do too much of what I want; the well-guided passages show the influence of my early readers, while any remaining bad ideas or bad taste in this book are mine.

I am so grateful to be able to work with Ave again. Kristi McDonald edited the manuscript with a sure touch, and Shannon Lee, working with Catherine Owers, provided thoughtful, thorough copyediting.

My confessors and my friends (especially Ratty) showed me great patience while I was working on this thing. And for the final stretch I was living with my parents, to whom I owe far more than any acknowledgments page can convey.

NOTES

INTRODUCTION

1. Parts of this introduction are adapted from a talk I gave at the Revoice conference in 2018.

2. If you want to read more about what brought me into the Church, it's the first several chapters of my previous book, *Gay and Catholic: Accepting My Sexuality, Finding Community, Living My Faith* (Notre Dame, IN: Ave Maria Press, 2014).

3. There are serious problems with any analogy between earthly hierarchies and spiritual ones. I don't mean to imply that the economic inequality between mistress and handmaiden, between homeowner and housekeeper, or between employer and maid is natural or good. Another possible analogy for our trust in God's message, as conveyed to us by the Church, might be Mary's trust in God's message as conveyed to her by the archangel Gabriel. She had to trust that this was no fallen angel full of lies, but a trustworthy messenger to whom she could give a wholehearted *yes*. Still, the imagery from the psalm shows a woman in authority, paralleling the many images of the Church as a woman. As our mother, the Church has authority greater than that of any human mother; as the Bride of Christ, she has an intimate knowledge of God's will, greater than the knowledge any human wife has of her husband. It is this intimacy with God that makes her authority trustworthy, not arbitrary.

1. THE GAY CATHOLIC DRINKING GAME

1. Arguably it *did* help send me to the hospital. I would've been an alcoholic anyway because it's fun at first, but I did not quite escape entirely unscathed from the terrible ways our churches have sought to "minister to" gay people. Well, nobody should want to live entirely unscathed while others suffer, I guess. Bottoms up!

2. Or in the words of Dr. James Dobson in his popular book *Preparing for Adolescence*, "Homosexuality is an abnormal desire that reflects deep

problems, but it doesn't happen very often and it's not likely to happen to you." James Dobson, *Preparing for Adolescence* (Ventura, CA: Regal Press, 1980), 89. Both Wesley Hill and Tim Otto, gay Christians living celibately, have cited this line as a searing and unforgettable lesson in what God had to offer them. For Hill see the foreword to Mark Yarhouse, *Understanding Sexual Identity: A Resource for Youth Ministry* (Grand Rapids, MI: Zondervan, 2013); for Otto, *Oriented to Faith: Transforming the Conversation over Gay Relationships* (Eugene, OR: Cascade Books, 2014).

3. For an especially powerful story of this kind, see Vicky Beeching's story of exorcism, shame, and life-threatening illness in Patrick Strudwick, "Vicky Beeching, Christian Rock Star: 'I'm Gay. God Loves Me Just the Way I Am,'" *The Independent* (UK), August 13, 2014, accessed June 26, 2020, https://www.independent.co.uk/news/people/news/vicky-beeching-star-of-the-christian-rock-scene-im-gay-god-loves-me-just-the-way-i-am-9667566.html.

4. This is real! Joseph Erbentraut, "Man's Disappearance Renews Debate on 'Ex-Gay' Netherworld," *EDGE Magazine*, August 10, 2009, https://boston.edgemedianetwork.com/index.php?ch=news&sc=&sc3=&id=94784&pg=2.

5. I'm sorry to keep using "straight" like this. I know I'm reifying a social construct and not a particularly kind one. But if it quacks like a duck . . . it reifies duckness. The best I can say is that very few of us entirely avoid quacking.

6. Payne's *The Broken Image: Restoring Personal Wholeness through Healing Prayer* treats being gay solely as a form of "brokenness" that results from past hurts and can be healed through prayer. "Healing" is defined as becoming heterosexual.

7. Verbatim from an interview with Ben Finger of Morehead City, NC.

8. The National Organization for Marriage (NOM). The large majority of people I worked with in this movement were unfailingly kind and thoughtful toward me; Maggie Gallagher, NOM's cofounder, has been a friend and mentor. Their kindness may, in fact, have made it harder for me to hear what others were telling me about the way opposition to gay marriage was playing out in ordinary churches and homes.

9. "Interview: LGBT Youth and Homelessness," *Spiritual Friendship,* August 17, 2015, accessed June 26, 2020, https://spiritualfriendship. org/2015/08/17/interview-lgbt-youth-and-homelessness/.

10. It's now deleted, but I credit Bridget Eileen Rivera with opening this conversation on her Twitter account. Stories poured in—all from people who thought they were the only ones these things had happened to.

11. See, for example, the experience Sarah describes in "50 Shades of Grey and the Dangers of Soundbite Sexual Ethics," *A Queer Calling,* February 23, 2015, accessed June 26, 2020, http://aqueer-calling.com/2015/02/23/50-shades-of-grey-and-the-dangers-of-sound-bite-sexual-ethics/.

12. This is not part of Sarah's story. It's something a different woman discussed with me in an interview.

13. See chapter 2, y'all.

2. SAME SEX LOVE

1. Dunstan Thompson, "Tarquin," in *Here at Last Is Love: Selected Poems of Dunstan Thompson,* ed. Gregory Wolfe (Eugene, OR: Wipf and Stock, 2015), 8.

2. Dana Gioia, "Two Poets Named Dunstan Thompson," *Hudson Review,* Spring 2015, accessed June 26, 2020, https://hudsonreview. com/2015/05/two-poets-named-dunstan-thompson/.

3. Thompson, "The Moment of the Rose," in *Here at Last Is Love,* 48.

4. As described in William Doino Jr., "A Witness, in Life and Letters," *First Things,* December 15, 2014, accessed April 19, 2021, https://www. firstthings.com/web-exclusives/2014/12/a-witness-in-life-and-letters.

5. Gregory Wolfe, introduction to *Here at Last Is Love,* xxvi–xxvii.

6. Doino, "A Witness, in Life and Letters."

7. Gioia, "Two Poets."

8. Wolfe, introduction to *Here at Last Is Love,* xxx.

9. Quoted in Gioia, "Two Poets."

10. Gioia, "Two Poets."

11. Gioia, afterword to *Here at Last Is Love,* 113.

12. Thompson, "Three Views of Assisi," in *Here at Last,* 64, and "The Halfway House," 73.

13. *Catechism of the Catholic Church*, 2nd ed. (Washington, DC: United States Catholic Conference, 2000), 2358.

14. Usually gay porn, while they were receiving "aversion therapy" in the form of electric shocks or emetic drugs. See, for example, Glenn Smith et al., "Treatments of Homosexuality in Britain since the 1950s—An Oral history: The Experience of Patients," *British Medical Journal*, February 21, 2004, accessed June 26, 2020, https://www.ncbi.nlm.nih.gov/pmc/articles/PMC344257/. An extreme example is the case of "B-19," given electric stimulation of the so-called pleasure center while watching straight porn. Christen M. O'Neal et al., "Dr. Robert G. Heath: A Controversial Figure in the History of Deep Brain Stimulation," *Journal of Neurosurgery* 43, no. 3 (September 2017), accessed June 26, 2020, https://thejns.org/focus/view/journals/neurosurg-focus/43/3/article-pE12.xml.

15. See, for example, Andrew Giambrone, "LGBTQ People Suffered Traumatic Treatments at St. Elizabeths Hospital for the Mentally Ill," *Washington City Paper*, May 31, 2018, accessed June 26, 2020, https://www.washingtoncitypaper.com/news/article/21007233/independent-scholars-uncover-the-traumatic-treatments-lgbtq-people-suffered-at-st-elizabeths.

16. This is an extreme simplification. The idea that there is a class of person who is inherently drawn to couple with someone of the same sex can be found at least as far back as the legend of the round people in Plato's *Symposium*, and there are hints of subcultures of men who preferred sex with men that predate the use of the term "homosexual"—see, for example, Tim Hitchcock, "Subcultures and Sodomites: The Development of Homosexuality," in *English Sexualities: 1700–1800* (London: Macmillan, 1997). But in the nineteenth century the idea of "homosexuality" as a condition attained widespread popularity that the earlier hints of this worldview never reached. For an overview of this development, see "Homosexuality," *Stanford Encyclopedia of Philosophy*, revised April 28, 2020, accessed June 26, 2020, https://plato.stanford.edu/entries/homosexuality/. The popularity of this pseudoscientific concept was largely due to the nineteenth-century passion for categorizing human variation in order to reduce it through medical treatment—don't @ me.

17. For real. See, for example, Robinson Meyer, "Alan Turing's Body," *The Atlantic*, December 26, 2013, accessed June 26, 2020, https://www.theatlantic.com/technology/archive/2013/12/alan-turings-body/282641/.

18. Though it was only the beginning of the end. Psychiatric theories about the "origin" and "healing" of homosexuality still mar many Christian ministries, including many Catholic institutions. See for example Eve Tushnet, "Conversion Therapy Is Still Happening in Catholic Spaces—And Its Effects on LGBT People Can Be Devastating," *America*, May 13, 2021, accessed June 9, 2021, https://www.americamagazine.org/faith/2021/05/13/conversion-therapy-lgbt-catholic-240635.

19. Ron Belgau, "Love, Covenant, and Friendship," *Spiritual Friendship*, September 15, 2015, accessed June 26, 2020, https://spiritualfriendship.org/2015/09/15/love-covenant-and-friendship/.

20. Both are quoted in the *Catechism of the Catholic Church* (Vatican City: Libreria Editrice Vaticana, 2005), 460, accessed June 26, 2020, http://www.vatican.va/archive/ENG0015/__P1J.HTM.

21. Back in *Gay and Catholic* I quoted the sublime passage on Jonathan's love in St. Aelred's *Spiritual Friendship*, so I won't repeat that quotation here. But if you want a meditation on Jonathan as prefiguration of Christ, as lord who humbles himself to exalt his friend, you can't do better than to read that passage. See Aelred of Rievaulx, *Spiritual Friendship* (Kalamazoo: Cistercian Publications, 1977), 115–17.

22. I'd cite the folk song, but I forgot the singer's name and I've never been able to find it on the Internet!

23. See, for example, Rebecca T. Alpert, *Like Bread on the Seder Plate: Jewish Lesbians and the Transformation of Tradition* (New York: Columbia University Press, 1997), 48; "20 Tips for the Perfect LGBTQ Wedding," *The Advocate*, March 19, 2019, accessed June 26, 2020, https://www.advocate.com/exclusives/2019/3/19/17-tips-perfect-lgbtq-wedding#-media-gallery-media-13.

24. Eve Tushnet, "Beyond Religious Life and Marriage: A Look at Friendship as Vocation," *America*, January 24, 2017, accessed June 26, 2020, https://www.americamagazine.org/faith/2017/01/24/beyond-religious-life-and-marriage-look-friendship-vocation.

25. And if you want a more scholarly treatment, I can't recommend Alan Bray's masterful *The Friend* (Chicago: University of Chicago Press, 2003) highly enough. He covers only English traditions, but he gives you a lyrical introduction to the ways Christian same-sex friendship could shape a life.

26. The examples we know of from history are almost exclusively male. Women usually lacked the control of their economic and domestic lives needed to shape those lives around their friendships, and they were also much less likely to have their choices recorded for posterity. This absence from the historical record makes Ruth and Naomi all the more poignant and necessary as models.

These friendships' obligations could be stricter in some respects than marital duties. Married couples in the Church don't promise to live together or share their money and goods. And their vowed obligations to one another end with the death of either of the spouses. Pledges of friendship, by contrast, often specified that the friends would become an economic unit—and that when one friend died, the other would pray and have Masses said for his soul, ensuring that their bond would remain even when one friend had gone to his reward.

27. Unlike with marriage, it never became customary to include a priest's blessing when making vows of friendship. However, some contemporary believers have sought blessings for their covenants from their priests. You don't have to—it isn't traditional!—but for some people it adds to the ceremony and solemnity of their pledge. In 2021 the Congregation for the Doctrine of the Faith (CDF) issued a statement warning that Catholic priests cannot bless "same-sex unions"—but the statement discusses only "relationships . . . that involve sexual activity outside of marriage," or which "constitute a certain analogue or imitation of the nuptial blessing." Responsum from the Congregation for the Doctrine of the Faith to a dubium regarding the blessing of the unions of persons of the same sex, February 22, 2021, available via the Catholic News Agency, accessed April 27, 2021, https://www.catholicnewsagency.com/news/246855/full-text-vaticans-doctrinal-office-response-and-note-on-the-blessing-of-same-sex-unions. On a pastoral level, it is noteworthy that the CDF goes out of its way to acknowledge "positive elements" in sexually active gay relationships—but then offers no suggestion as to how these positive elements might be preserved and even deepened in a life conformed to Catholic teaching, which we trust is always a life of deeper love. On a personal level, if you're a Catholic seeking or living within a covenant friendship that is not intended to be sexual or marital, and you'd like a priest's blessing, it's my best judgment that the CDF statement does

not address your situation, and your priest has no reason to hesitate in blessing your union.

28. A term people understand in various ways, as we try to work out how to live our lives. See Tushnet, "Beyond Religious Life and Marriage."

29. See, for example, Kay Hymowitz et al., "Knot Yet: The Benefits and Costs of Delayed Marriage in America," accessed June 26, 2020, http://nationalmarriageproject.org/wordpress/wp-content/uploads/2013/04/KnotYet-FinalForWeb-041413.pdf.

30. Janet Adamy, "U.S. Marriage Rate Plunges to Lowest Level on Record," *Wall Street Journal*, April 29, 2020.

31. Meg Baatz, "Aiming Higher/Burdens Lighter," in Bill Henson, *Guiding Families of LGBT+ Loved Ones,* 2nd ed. (Acton, MA: Posture Shift Books, 2018), 109.

32. Aaron Taylor, "'Chaste, Gay Couples' and the Church," *Spiritual Friendship*, February 4, 2015, accessed June 26, 2020, https://spiritual-friendship.org/2015/02/04/chaste-gay-couples-and-the-church/.

33. David Foster Wallace, *Infinite Jest*, 20th anniversary edition (New York: Little, Brown, 2016), 274.

34. Robert Sarah, *The Power of Silence: Against the Dictatorship of Noise* (San Francisco, CA: Ignatius Press, 2017), 44–45.

35. Sarah, *Power of Silence*, 45.

36. Available at, for example, Liturgies.net, accessed April 17, 2021, http://www.liturgies.net/saints/john/morningprayer.htm.

3. THE SECRET GARDEN

1. This chapter is adapted from a talk I gave at the 2018 Revoice conference.

2. Quoted in Xavier Bray et al., *The Sacred Made Real: Spanish Painting and Sculpture 1600–1700* (London: National Gallery, 2009), 162.

3. This paragraph is quoted directly from a previous article I wrote, "Intimacy, Joy and Relief: A Painting That Reveals the Heart of Penance," *Catholic Herald*, December 13, 2018, accessed June 27, 2020, https://catholicherald.co.uk/magazine/portraying-the-quiet-joy-of-penance/.

4. "Black Nun Pleads for 'God-Convicted Women,'" *Pittsburgh Courier*, December 5, 1970, 5.

5. Don Seeman et al., "Blessing Unintended Pregnancy: Religion and the Discourse of Women's Agency in Public Health," *Medicine Anthropology Theory*, April 14, 2016, accessed June 27, 2020, http://www.medan-throtheory.org/read/6056/blessing-unintended-pregnancy.

6. Archdiocese of Philadelphia, *Love Is Our Mission: The Family Fully Alive, A Preparatory Catechesis for the World Meeting of Families* (Huntington, IN: Our Sunday Visitor, 2014), 67, accessed June 27, 2020, https://www.dio.org/uploads/files/Marriage_and_Family_Life/Love_Is_Our_Mission/LoveisOurMission_final_pdf.pdf.

7. See Otto, *Oriented to Faith*, and *A Queer Calling*, updated January 21, 2017, accessed June 27, 2020, http://aqueercalling.com/. The blog isn't being updated mostly because the authors felt they'd said what they had to say about their partnership.

8. This section is adapted from my post, "'The Body & Society' Notes Pt 1: Damned to Pixar Heaven," *Patheos*, January 19, 2018, accessed June 27, 2020, https://www.patheos.com/blogs/evetushnet/2018/01/body-society-notes-pt-1-damned-pixar-heaven.html.

9. Peter Brown, *The Body and Society: Men, Women, and Sexual Renunciation in Early Christianity* (New York: Columbia University Press, 1988), 286.

10. I got this from Kyle Harper, *From Shame to Sin: The Christian Transformation of Sexual Morality in Late Antiquity* (Cambridge, MA: Harvard University Press, 2013), 269n60, but it's from Methodius's *Symposium* for more scholarly types who want to find it in its natural habitat.

11. See, for example, Kim Parker and Renee Stepler, "As U.S. Marriage Rate Hovers at 50%, Education Gap in Marital Status Widens," *Pew Research Center*, September 14, 2017, accessed June 27, 2020, https://www.pewresearch.org/fact-tank/2017/09/14/as-u-s-marriage-rate-hovers-at-50-education-gap-in-marital-status-widens/.

12. Christopher C. Roberts, *Creation and Covenant: The Significance of Sexual Difference in the Moral Theology of Marriage* (London: T&T Clark International, 2007), 245.

13. Roberts, *Creation and Covenant*, 227.

14. Brown, *Body and Society*, 67.

15. Brown, *Body and Society*, 101–2.

16. Aelred had been in some way unchaste before entering monastic life, and this was widely known; see "Walter Daniel's Letter to Maurice,"

in Walter Daniel, *The Life of Saint Aelred* (Kalamazoo, MI: Cistercian Publications, 1994), 154.

17. Quoted in Caroline Walker Bynum, *Jesus as Mother: Studies in the Spirituality of the High Middle Ages* (Berkeley and Los Angeles, CA: University of California Press, 1982), 188.

4. WEAPONIZED CHRISTIANITY

1. Elaine Scarry, *The Body in Pain: The Making and Unmaking of the World* (New York: Oxford University Press, 1985), 41.

2. "Waterboarding Survivors Speak Out," *Stop Torture*, November 10, 2007, accessed June 27, 2020, https://blogs.harvard.edu/stoptorture/2007/11/10/waterboarding-survivors-speak-out/. I made the same comparison between Scarry and St. Francis in "Theology of the Body in Pain," *Crisis*, February 12, 2008.

3. Elena, "Jesus Is Not an Abusive Boyfriend," in *Christ's Body, Christ's Wounds: Staying Catholic When You've Been Hurt in the Church*, ed. Eve Tushnet (Eugene, OR: Wipf and Stock, 2018), 26–28.

4. James Martin, S.J., *Building a Bridge: How the Catholic Church and the LGBT Community Can Enter into a Relationship of Respect, Compassion, and Sensitivity* (New York: HarperCollins, 2017), 109–12. (Martin quotes the NRSV translation of Psalm 139.)

5. Martin, *Building a Bridge*, 112.

6. With apologies to *Saturday Night Live*.

7. Ralph Ellison, *Juneteenth* (New York: Random House, 1999), 201.

8. The *Symposium* rises, of course, to Socrates's image of the "ladder of love," suggesting that even for these soulmate couples, sexual acts are not the best expression of their love and not the best response to the beauty they rightly perceive in each other. But for the purposes of the less-important argument about whether "homosexuality" is a cultural construct, Aristophanes's speech about the round people is the relevant bit.

9. Harper, *From Shame to Sin*, 35.

10. I admit that I made this joke already, in "The Naked Emperors," *The University Bookman*, April 15, 2018, accessed June 27, 2020, https://kirkcenter.org/reviews/the-naked-emperors/.

5. IF I'M CELIBATE, CAN I STILL FLIRT WITH ANGER?

1. Paul Flynn and Matthew Todd, "Pride and Prejudice for Gay Men," *The Guardian*, February 19, 2011, accessed June 26, 2020, https://www.theguardian.com/society/2011/feb/20/gay-men-depression-the-velvet-rage.

2. Chris Damian, "I Tell You for Mercy," personal blog, April 9, 2019, accessed June 29, 2020, https://chrisdamian.net/2019/04/09/i-tell-you-for-mercy/.

3. Chris Damian wrote another good post on his path through anger toward peace: "I've Been Mad at the Church," personal blog, July 3, 2018, accessed June 29, 2020, https://chrisdamian.net/2018/07/03/ive-been-mad-at-the-church/.

6. IT'S THE SODOM AND GOMORRAH SHOW! SEX, SHAME, AND HOPE

1. Saraphernalia, Twitter, July 21, 2018, accessed June 29, 2020, https://twitter.com/saraphernalia/statuses/1020881997080793088.

2. A year and five months, and I'm glad to say I am no longer counting the specific weeks.

3. Chris Damian, "Gay Celibacy, Step One," personal blog, March 6, 2018, accessed June 29, 2020, https://chrisdamian.net/2018/03/06/gay-celibacy-step-one/.

4. An analogy might be drawn with the theologian James H. Cone's description of the role hard-partying, blues-blaring "juke joints" played in the souls of Southern black people. The juke joint wasn't a place his churchgoing mother would let her children go, and yet the juke joint flowed with joy and laughter because it was a site of liberation. At the juke joint even songs about black men's sexual prowess could hide an assertion of self-respect: *I am a man.* The juke joint can't offer the fullness of liberation, only scraps and seeds; but desperate people will make a meal of scraps and seeds. Cone adds, "Unlike the spirituals and the church, the blues and the juke joint did not lead to organized political resistance against white supremacy. . . . The blues prepared people to fight for justice by giving them a cultural identity that made them human and thus ready to struggle. The blues sent people traveling, roaming, looking for a woman

or a man to soothe one's aching human heart. But it was Jesus' cross that sent people protesting in the streets, seeking to change the social structures of racial oppression." James H. Cone, *The Cross and the Lynching Tree* (Maryknoll, NY: Orbis Books, 2011), 16–17, 28.

5. Chris Damian, "Catholicism, Pornography, and Homosexuality," personal blog, May 23, 2018, accessed June 29, 2020, https://chrisdamian.net/2018/05/23/catholicism-pornography-and-homosexuality/.

6. I owe this insight to the *Clerically Speaking* podcast, where several people in religious vows discussed how the desire for validation can push people into unchastity, inappropriate emotional entanglements, or the many attention-seeking dangers of social media. "Episode 93: Religious Chastity/No Summa?/Sr. Theresa," *Clerically Speaking*, accessed April 27, 2021, https://soundcloud.com/user-931742388/e93-religious-chastity-no-suma-sr-theresa. My vague memory is that there's a brief digression into specifically gay questions, which isn't as good as it should be, but I appreciated the way the hosts and guest connected unchastity to other disordered expressions of the same yearning.

7. Brown, *The Body and Society*, 238.

8. Brown, *Body and Society*, 232–34.

9. E. V. Debs, "Statement to the Court upon Being Convicted of Violating the Sedition Act," September 18, 1918, accessed June 29, 2020, https://www.marxists.org/archive/debs/works/1918/court.htm. I bet you weren't expecting *that* domain name to show up in this book.

10. Quoted in Edward Mendelson, *Early Auden, Later Auden: A Critical Biography* (Princeton, NJ: Princeton University Press, 2017), 749.

11. I'm thinking here of people whose sins of lust are not accompanied by sins of abuse of their power over others. When you're abusing your power over others in order to satisfy your sexual urges, I suspect it is hard to be either honest or humble about what you're doing.

12. This section is adapted from my blog post "The Body & Society Notes Part 6 . . . I Think: Blessed Are the Sleazoids," *Patheos*, February 8, 2018, accessed June 29, 2020, https://www.patheos.com/blogs/evetushnet/2018/02/body-society-notes-part-6-think-blessed-sleazoids.html.

7. AMBIVALENCE

1. Stephen Rollnick and William Richard Miller, *Motivational Interviewing, Third Edition: Helping People Change* (New York: Guilford Press, 2013), 6.

2. Rollnick and Miller, *Motivational Interviewing*, 234.

3. Tim Otto writes powerfully in *Oriented to Faith* about his decision to accept celibacy, and even take a vow of celibacy, despite the fact that he isn't convinced by his church's interpretation of scripture. That vow didn't include a vow to shut up about his beliefs! See Tim Otto, *Oriented to Faith: Transforming the Conversation over Gay Relationships* (Eugene, OR: Cascade Books, 2014).

8. LOVE'S BEEN A LITTLE BIT HARD ON ME

1. A lot of studies have found this, but I'm relying on the Trevor Project's citation of the Centers for Disease Control, "Sexual Identity, Sex of Sexual Contacts, and Health-Risk Behaviors Among Students in Grades 9–12: Youth Risk Behavior Surveillance" (Atlanta, GA: U.S. Department of Health and Human Services, 2016). Cited by the Trevor Project, accessed April 30, 2021, https://www.thetrevorproject.org/resources/preventing-suicide/facts-about-suicide/.

2. Anne Harding, "Religious Faith Linked to Suicidal Behavior in LGBQ Adults," *Reuters Health*, April 13, 2018, accessed April 30, 2021, https://www.reuters.com/article/us-health-lgbq-religion-suicide/religious-faith-linked-to-suicidal-behavior-in-lgbq-adults-idUSKBN1HK-2MA.

3. Several sentences and phrases in this passage are quoted or adapted from Tushnet, *Gay and Catholic*, 200–01.

4. I know you want to tell me, "But Eve, they don't mean 'happiness' like 'good feelings'! They mean *eudaimonia*—human flourishing. It's sort of like happiness except that it can feel bad!" My friend, will eudaimonia pay the rent? Will it keep me warm at night?

5. Quoted in Eamon Duffy, *John Henry Newman: A Very Brief History* (London: Society for Promoting Christian Knowledge, 2019), 79.

9. COME OUT, COME OUT, WHEREVER YOU ARE!

1. Gregg Webb, "Ten Years," *Eleison Blog*, November 23, 2019, accessed July 1, 2020, https://eleisonblog.org/2019/11/23/ten-years/.

10. ADMIRE A HOMOSEXUAL FOR JESUS

1. In my view, pressuring people to call themselves "same-sex attracted" rather than "gay" also separates people from gay communities, discouraging them from identifying with or even getting to know gay people. That doesn't mean "same-sex attracted" is never a valid way to understand your situation. I've known several people who found that language helpful, in the short- or long-term. I'm speaking here to well-meaning priests and other spiritual guides who have tried to impose this language on others without understanding what it might cost them.

2. Cone, *The Cross and the Lynching Tree*, 146.

11. LEAD, KINDLY LIGHT

1. Sorry for this jargon. It's a term typically used to signify Christians, most often LGBT Christians, who accept their churches' teaching that sex is reserved for marriage between one man and one woman. Someday we'll come up with a shorthand I actually like.

14. BEING OF SERVICE

1. I wrote a bit more about this discernment process, and about the ways my experience at the center has shaped my understanding of gay Christian life, in *Gay and Catholic: Accepting My Sexuality, Finding Community, Living My Faith* (Notre Dame, IN: Ave Maria Press, 2014).

2. Steve shared this reflection with me in a personal email.

15. 2 FAST 2 FABULOUS

1. St. Basil the Great, "First Homily on Fasting," translated by Kent Burghius, Orthodox Christian Campus Ministries, accessed July 1, 2020, http://rutgersnb.occministries.org/wp-content/uploads/2015/07/St.-Basil-the-Great%E2%80%99s-First-Homily-on-Fasting.pdf.

2. With apologies, again, to *Saturday Night Live*.

3. Eamon Duffy, "To Fast Again," *First Things*, March 2005, accessed July 1, 2020, https://www.firstthings.com/article/2005/03/to-fast-again

16. IT'S HIS BODY AND I'LL CRY IF I WANT TO

1. I had an experience at adoration once, which I'm relegating to a footnote because I realize it might just be psychological. But I was aware of how much I was controlled by a particular besetting sin. I was bowing my head, on my knees, thinking I was praying ardently, when I felt something. Not a physical force, but something *like* a physical force: an impetus, a pressure from outside, below my chin, lifting my head so that I looked at Jesus in the Eucharist. I think he wanted me to know that nothing in my life could keep him from wanting to see my face.

17. ALL THE NAMES OF GOD

1. All of the above from Caroline Walker Bynum, "Jesus as Mother and Abbot as Mother: Some Themes in Twelfth-Century Cistercian Writing," in Bynum, *Jesus as Mother: Studies in the Spirituality of the High Middle Ages* (Berkeley and Los Angeles, CA: University of California Press, 1982), esp. 112–25 and 141–42.

2. Wesley Hill, *The Lord's Prayer: A Guide to Praying to Our Father* (Bellingham, WA: Lexham Press, 2019), 99–101.

FURTHER READING

The following books have helped shape my understanding of the issues discussed in this book. It's a quirky list, and not a comprehensive one. When I wrote *Gay and Catholic* it was possible, even easy, to read pretty much all the books by gay people about living out the Christian sexual ethic. Now, thank God, with so many more such books available, that's a big task—which I admit I shirked. So these are a mere selection, focusing on the books that discuss the themes of this book rather than other issues pertinent to gay Christian life.

Aelred of Rievaulx. *Spiritual Friendship.*
> Dialogues on Christian friendship that are at once practical, challenging, and beautiful. Aelred's understanding of friendship as imitation of Christ reshaped my thinking, and arguably my life. You might also check out Walter Daniel's *Life of Aelred of Rievaulx*—Daniel was one of Aelred's monks and is in fact the "Walter" in the *Spiritual Friendship* dialogues, a fact of which he's endearingly proud.

Archdiocese of Philadelphia. *Love Is Our Mission: The Family Fully Alive.*
> A sort of mini-catechism that weaves celibate people and our relationships into the fabric of a parish community in a way few similar documents even attempt.

Bernard of Clairvaux. *Sermons on the Song of Songs.*
> If you want "bridal mysticism" (mystical contemplation of the soul as bride of Christ) straight up, no mixers, you can get it here. A truly medieval mind: rapt in Christ, obsessed with symbolism, bizarre, and tender.

Bray, Alan. *The Friend.*
   A study of publicly recognized same-sex friendship in England
   from the medieval era to the age of St. John Newman. Heartfelt,
   full of potential models for us, and also very aware that new
   beauties can create new temptations and new social problems.

Brown, Peter. *The Body and Society: Men, Women, and Sexual
Renunciation in Early Christianity.*
   A fountain of examples . . . and, occasionally, cautionary tales.
   Connects sexual renunciation to Christian belief in the afterlife
   and to the Christian challenge to the Roman economic structure. Frequently beautiful, both in Brown's own writing and in
   those he quotes, as well as nuanced and sympathetic.

Cameli, Fr. Louis J. *Catholic Teaching on Homosexuality: New Paths
to Understanding.*
   A highly abstract but imaginative and provocative attempt to
   suggest ways in which gay people can experience our sexuality
   as a blessing, within the Catholic sexual ethic.

Coles, Gregory. *Single, Gay, Christian: A Personal Journey of Faith
and Sexual Identity.*
   A short, charming memoir and reflection on friendship in
   scripture. This is a relatively light expression of the angst that
   comes from even a gentle and well-intentioned upbringing in
   contemporary American evangelicalism; it also explores the
   early stages of the path through that angst to a deeper trust in
   God, acceptance of oneself, and delight in the forms of love
   Christ has modeled for you.

Damian, Christopher. "A Catholic Perspective on Homoerotic Desire," *Logos: A Journal of Catholic Thought and Culture*, vol. 22, issue 1.

A provocative and fruitful attempt to work out the meaning of homoerotic desire through the thought of Popes John Paul II and Benedict XVI.

Downs, Alan. *The Velvet Rage: Overcoming the Pain of Growing Up Gay in a Straight Man's World.*

I'm not sure why I feel the need to say, "I didn't think his prescriptions were as universally applicable as he seems to," since none of these books are universally applicable. But if you read this with a willingness to "take what you need and leave the rest," as they say in AA, it may help you to treat yourself and others better, by working honestly through pain.

Henson, Bill, *Guiding Families of LGBT+ Loved Ones.*

This book comes from the Lead Them Home ministry, which helps what I would describe as conservative Protestants accept and cherish their LGBT (etc.) children. It includes personal reflections from parents, from LGBT people ourselves, from straight ministers, from gay ministers . . . just a wide variety of perspectives, all aimed at increasing our understanding and ability to love one another. I have some criticisms, and parts of this book may be a painful read for gay people since it does have to delve into the pain many parents experience when a child comes out. But this is a good starting point for pastors and parents.

Hill, Wesley. *Spiritual Friendship: Finding Love in the Church as a Celibate Gay Christian.*

A personal, literary reflection on building deeper friendships in a culture—including a church culture—that doesn't quite know how to support them.

Hill, Wesley. *Washed and Waiting: Reflections on Christian Faithfulness and Homosexuality.*

Memoir, scriptural reflection, and search for role models—Hill's first book shows a young heart trying to understand God's faithfulness in a world where refuge seemed terribly hard to find. I found the reflections on loneliness deeply consoling, but I'm glad this is no longer almost the only book to recommend, and I am sure Wes would agree.

Martin, Fr. James, S.J. *Building a Bridge: How the Catholic Church and the LGBT Community Can Enter into a Relationship of Respect, Compassion, and Sensitivity.*

The first half of this book is mostly about the relationship between Catholic leaders and those LGBT people who no longer practice the faith (or never did). The second half, however, offers reflections on scripture that would be valuable for the readers of this book and, if they're open to it, your families.

Otto, Tim. *Oriented to Faith: Transforming the Conflict over Gay Relationships.*

A slender book about coming out, struggling with scripture and self-hatred, discovering a complicated peace in a Christian intentional community, and taking a vow of celibacy to remain there. Maybe the only gay Christian memoir that explores the way Christian faith and community should reshape our economic and political priorities.

de Pougy, Liane. *My Blue Notebooks: The Intimate Journal of Paris's Most Beautiful and Notorious Courtesan.*

Don't you want to read it already? This is the diary of a woman who went from infamous bisexual adventuress to lay Dominican. You get to watch a very candid soul swing wildly back and forth between love of this world and love of God. Fair warning, her worldliness includes casual anti-Semitism and class prejudice; unlike her materialism and sexual decadence, she doesn't quite recognize these things as sins, although she does seem to outgrow them as her spiritual life deepens.

Rapp, Claudia. *Brother-Making in Late Antiquity and Byzantium: Monks, Laymen, and Christian Ritual.*
A careful, scholarly exploration of the monastic origin and spiritual purposes of Eastern Christian rituals uniting unrelated adults as siblings. Like Bray, Rapp shows you both the beauties of "brother-making" and the ways it can go wrong; she makes it clear that this Eastern tradition is distinct from the Western traditions of vowed friendship explored by Bray.

Rivera, Bridget Eileen. *Heavy Burdens: Seven Ways LGBTQ Christians Experience Harm in the Church.*
Explores in greater depth and context many of the experiences I described in chapter 1. I cannot endorse all of Bridget's proposals (this may be the most Protestant book I've ever read!), but she lets LGBTQ Christians tell their stories in their own words: stories our churches urgently need to hear. She also drops some much-needed knowledge about the ways racism and colonialism shape anti-gay Christianity.

Swan, Laura. *The Wisdom of the Beguines: The Forgotten Story of a Medieval Women's Movement.*
Written for a normal, nonscholarly audience, this book tells the story of medieval and early modern laywomen who banded together in communities of prayer, service, and labor. The beguines, like contemporary gay Christian movements, even managed to cross the lines dividing Catholic and Protestant. This book is a little too partisan and dismisses any possibility that beguines could cause real problems, but as an easily readable picture of communal Christian life outside the monastery it's hard to beat.

Thompson, Dunstan. *Here at Last Is Love: Selected Poems of Dunstan Thompson.*
> Includes Dana Gioia's essay as well as all of the poetry I've quoted in this book. Editor Gregory Wolfe's selections highlight the transformation that love and Christ worked in Thompson's poetry.

Tushnet, Eve, ed. *Christ's Body, Christ's Wounds: Staying Catholic When You've Been Hurt in the Church.*
> This anthology offers essays and poetry reflecting on the spiritual aspects of recovery from harms experienced in our churches. There's one specifically gay entry, but I'm listing the book here because the array of perspectives on healing and reshaping your faith may be useful to you.

Tushnet, Eve. *Gay and Catholic: Accepting My Sexuality, Finding Community, Living My Faith.*
> If you liked this book, you might like its predecessor. You get my conversion story plus an exploration of some of the pathways of love that are open to gay people in the Catholic Church.

I understand that the "youth of today" learn primarily through podcasts. *Life on Side B* is a wide-ranging podcast, available at LifeonSideB.com. They've touched on celibacy in community, mental health and loneliness, racial justice, queer Christian solidarity, prayer, race and cultural difference, and much more.

EVE TUSHNET is a freelance writer, a *Patheos* blogger, and the award-winning author of *Gay and Catholic*. She also has written two novels, is the editor of the anthology *Christ's Body, Christ's Wounds*, and has contributed to several books, including *Sex and the Spiritual Life*.

Tushnet has written on the paths of love available to gay Christians for a wide range of publications, including *America, American Conservative, Commonweal,* and *Christianity Today,* and online for *Atlantic, New York Times,* and *Washington Post.* She has spoken at multiple conferences for LGBT Christians. She also writes and speaks on the arts.

Tushnet lives in Washington, DC.

ALSO BY
EVE TUSHNET

Gay and Catholic
Accepting My Sexuality, Finding Community, Living My Faith

In this first book from an openly lesbian and celibate Catholic, Eve Tushnet recounts her spiritual and intellectual journey from atheist to faithful Catholic and shows how gay Catholics can love and be loved while adhering to Church teaching.

Eve Tushnet was among the unlikeliest of converts. Raised in a secular family, Tushnet was a typical Yale undergraduate until the day she went out to poke fun at a gathering of philosophical debaters, many of whom happened also to be Catholic. Instead of enjoying mocking what she termed the "zoo animals," she found herself engaged in intellectual conversation with them and, in a move that surprised even her, she soon converted to Catholicism. Already self-identifying as a lesbian, Tushnet searched for a third way in the seeming two-option system available to gay Catholics: reject Church teaching on homosexuality or reject the truth of your sexuality. *Gay and Catholic* is the fruit of Tushnet's searching: what she learned in studying Christian history and theology and her articulation of how gay Catholics can pour their love and need for connection into friendships, community, service, and artistic creation.

"Honest, fresh, and tremendously helpful, Eve Tushnet's book offers a roadmap for Catholics experiencing same-sex attraction."
—Brandon Vogt
Author of *Saints and Social Justice*